An Awakened Passion

Del Beyer

Copyright © 2016 by Delbert Beyer

All rights reserved.

No part of this book may be reproduced or distributed in any printed or electronic form without permission except in the case of brief quotations, embodied critical articles and reviews. Please do not participate in or encourage piracy of copyrighted materials in violation of author's rights.

ISBN 13: 9781539912552

ISBN 10: 539912558

Table of Contents

Acknowledgements …..Page 7
Quotations …..Page 9
Forward …..Page 11

Part 1: Historical Documents…..Page 15

The Declaration of Independence …..Page 16
Transcription of the 1789 Joint Resolution of Congress …..Page 26
The U. S. Bill of Rights …..Page 31
The Constitution of the United States: A Transcription …..Page 36
The Constitution Amendments …..Page 62

Part 2: Our Caravan Blog Articles…..Page 77

The "We the People" Map …..Page 78
Liberty Is Our Most Important Word …..Page 82
You and I Will pay the Piper …..Page 84
History of Uncle Sam Page 86
America's Uncle Sam Hospitalized …..Page 88
My Inner Voice …..Page 90
A Nuclear Senate Reinstatement provides A Two Year Window of Security …..Page 93
The President, Immigration Law, Constitutional Law and the Supreme Court …..Page 96
How Do You Kill 11 Million People? …..Page 99
The State of the Union That You Will Not Hear Tonight …..Page 101
Demagogues and Economics …..Page 105
Advice from Our 1st American to President Obama …..Page 107
The Past Has Always Gone On Before Us …..Page 111
Supreme Court Justices Should Have Term Limits …..Page 119
Slavery, War, Immigration as the Rule of Law …..Page 123
Three Questions for Your Consideration …..Page 129
Freedom: Past, Present and Future …..Page 130
A Progressive is too Big to Swallow …..Page 132

Woodrow Wilson's Progressive Legacy In Question …..Page 136
Enter Stage Left …..Page 138
Truth as a Journey on a Winding Road …..Page 141
The Electoral College …..Page 146
Progressives versus Truth in Trump Campaign …..Page 153
Free Speech Is an Unalienable Right …..Page 155
Choose Wisely ….. Page 157
About the Author…..Page 161

Acknowledgements

Just as no man is an island so it is that no writer writes alone. Loved ones, good friends, even the voices that only the writer hears contribute a different perspective or a suggestion to be shared and listened to. Collectively they have joined hands and hearts to stimulate the writing task I had assigned to myself. Their support and suggestions will never be seen or felt by those who read this writer's words but they are always present.

So it is that I gratefully acknowledge those voices and those kind and loving people who have surrounded and supported me and my dream to put our founding documents and personal thoughts into the hands of others so that they might understand the magnitude of the map created by our nation's founders for them.

My wife, Marilyn, has read and reread every word I have written and has listened patiently to every spoken word of frustration, fear and hope I have uttered and with a soft voice often suggested a better way.

My daughter, Kimberly, an impressively successful and diverse writer herself, has step by step encouraged and directed me toward the creation of my blog and the publication of this book not necessarily just for you the reader. She strongly urged me to gather my values and thoughts as a gift to my grandchildren.

My son, Brian, is a valuable asset to you and me because he has a keen sense of the importance of verbal simplicity. Lots of very big and important sounding words have gone to the office shredder because he said "Too complicated" and "You do want them to read this, right?"

My friend, Roger, is a man I have known for over forty years. He is the person I have most often asked, "What do you think?" He has been too kind much too often but he has often pointed to something and simply said "I don't understand what you are trying to say."

No book is complete without an appealing jacket and my son-in-law, Mike, has created a design which I believe is both appropriate and aesthetically appealing to the eye and for that I am grateful.

Last but certainly not least are the people who have stopped me on the street, in a grocery store or even a physical therapy site to utter the grandest words I have ever heard beside I love you. Those words in various ways all said thank you for reminding us of what is important and is ours to keep or lose.

"If history were taught in the form of stories, it would never be forgotten."
>	*Rudyard Kipling*

At the close of the Constitutional Convention on September 17, 1787 as Benjamin Franklin left the hall in Philadelphia, he was asked "What kind of government have you given us, Dr. Franklin?" He replied, "A republic if you can keep it."
>	*Benjamin Franklin*

"Democracy while it lasts is more bloody than either aristocracy or monarchy. Remember, democracy never lasts long. It soon wastes, exhausts and murders itself. There is never a democracy that did not commit suicide."
>	*John Adams*

"America will never be destroyed from the outside. If we falter and lose our freedoms, it will be because we destroyed ourselves."
>	*Abraham Lincoln*

Seven Deadly Sins
"I don't think."
"I don't know."
"I don't Care."
"I'm too busy."
"I leave well enough alone."
"I have no time to read and find out."
"I am not interested."
William John Henry Boetcker

"The truth is not for all men but only for those who seek it."
Ayn Rand

"The most common way people give up their power is by thinking they don't have any."
Alice Walker

Foreword

The book you are now holding was not intended to be a book. It was originally intended as a printed copy of our nation's historical documents to be presented as a gift from my wife and me.

I was hoping to be assisted not by Fed Ex or UPS but by our local newspaper. It was our local newspaper which would print it and deliver it to the homes of all of my neighbors. I literally wanted every person in my hometown who read the local newspaper to have the opportunity to hold and hopefully read and understand their very own copy of The Declaration of Independence, the Constitution of the United States, the Bill of Rights and the remaining seventeen Amendments to the Constitution. Collectively, these documents are the maps leading us to the liberty created by the founders and my fellow citizens are the modern day versions of the "We the People" described in the opening lines of the Constitution of the United States. I believe we all deserve the opportunity to hold, read and understand the maps. *It is both our right and our responsibility.*

Quite understandably, the newspaper's Editor trumped my naive enthusiasm with down to earth economic common sense. His unexpected real kindness changed the original goal but quietly opened another door.

By giving me his personal column space one Saturday morning in 2013, he bought into the heart of what I was trying to accomplish. With one simple action, he pointed me toward another way to begin to provide the maps. I soon learned that I could still speak directly to the people. I simply adopted a different way to remind them what was rightfully theirs and help them to understand that no part of freedom is free.

From July 4, 1776 to July 4, 2016 is 240 years. If we presume a new generation appears among us roughly every twenty years then fully twelve generations of human beings have contributed to United States history in that 240 years. Each of those generations contributed what they felt was necessary to make us free and keep us free.

How close have we come? Are we inching closer or will we miss the mark? I am concerned that my generation, born in the crisis of a great depression and a world war, will pass into history in the grasp of a perceived greater crisis. I believe we are becoming a nation without guiding principles and values or an understanding of who we are and what made us great. There is a growing chance that the great experiment of our founders will pass away, never to return.

Neil Douglas Klotz has suggested that we might think of time as a Caravan.

If he is accurate, today we all stand in the middle of our own personal caravans. The oldest moments of our self and shared histories have gone on before us. Behind us comes the future. What has happened and what will happen are simply parts of now. You and I are merely extensions of the people who have gone on before us into the arms of remembered and forgotten history. Together, we must make a connection to that past and understand its impact on our very near future.

Several years ago I found myself uncomfortable with and for my country. I value the nation's founders and I considered possible ways I could join hands and minds with those giants who have passed into history. What was so important to them that they risked everything to achieve the unthinkable? Could I learn to better understand the contents of the maps? Could I help others to do it too? Not to speak against the reality of that coalescing historical change bearing down upon us all is like burying my head in the sand.

I believe the rising crisis which I anticipate is totally preventable but only if we understand how and why this nation was given birth and has survived. I also believe the giants from our past wisely left us word maps. The maps are written guides generated from the Founder's experiences in the wilderness of a life without liberty and those maps need to be reclaimed and relearned.

Those who understand the maps understand the way out of present and future misery. Collectively, the maps can reinstall our inner compass and return our sense of purpose. They are the original gifts that keep on giving.

About a year ago, the ever present encouragement and support of my daughter gently nudged me from letters to the editor toward the vast web net as a way to reach out to you and others beyond the borders of my hometown.

The creation of a personal blog site became my next logical step toward a long sought destination. My goal to present the gift of history to others remained unfinished and the blog led me to yet another way to look at our nation's hard earned history.

Our Caravan, my blog, has proven to be a broad opportunity and a weighty responsibility. I must continue to learn from and accurately share identified historical truths which offer the possibility of a better future for all of us.

I am pleased that you are here. I hope you will learn something new and enjoy the journey.

Part 1: HISTORICAL DOCUMENTS

Keep in mind that these documents are copies of the original word maps created by our Founders and shown here. You will encounter original spellings and word choices which have historically evolved and changed. You will see capitalized words you think are mistakes. Each capitalized word from the original documents appears as written.

I value our nation's original and amended documents, our history, the philosophy of constitutional conservatism, the importance of governmental and personal economic responsibility and a safe and secure future for myself, my family, my children's families and all peoples who are citizens or are actively learning to become citizens.

The Declaration of Independence

Adopted in Congress 4 July 1776
The Unanimous Declaration of the Thirteen United States of America

When, in the Course of human events, it becomes necessary for one people to dissolve the political bands which have connected them with another, and to assume among the powers of the earth, the separate and equal station to which the Laws of Nature and of Nature's God entitle them, a decent respect to the opinions of mankind requires that they should declare the causes which impel them to the separation.

We hold these truths to be self-evident, that all men are created equal, that they are endowed by their Creator with certain unalienable Rights, that among these are Life, Liberty and the pursuit of Happiness. ---That to secure these rights, governments are instituted among men, deriving their just powers from the consent of the governed. That whenever any Form of Government becomes destructive of these ends, it is the Right of the People to alter or to abolish it, and to institute new Government, laying its foundation on such principles and organizing its powers in such form,as to them shall seem most likely to effect their Safety and Happiness. Prudence, indeed, will dictate that governments long established should not be changed for light and transient causes; and accordingly all experience hath shewn that mankind are more disposed to suffer, while evils are sufferable, than to right themselves by abolishing the forms to which they are accustomed. But when a long train of abuses and usurpations, pursuing invariably the same Object evinces a design to reduce them under absolute Despotism, it is their right, it is their duty, to throw off such government, and to provide new guards for their future security. -- Such has been the patient sufferance of these Colonies; and such is now the necessity which constrains them to alter their former Systems of Government. The history of the present King of Great Britain is a history of repeated injuries and usurpations, all having in direct object the establishment of an absolute Tyranny over these states. To prove this, let Facts be submitted to a candid world.

He has refused his Assent to Laws, the most wholesome and necessary for the public good.

He has forbidden his Governors to pass Laws of immediate and pressing importance, unless suspended in their operation till his Assent should be obtained; and when so suspended, he has utterly neglected to attend to them.

He has refused to pass other Laws for the accommodation of large districts of people, unless those people would relinquish the right of Representation in the Legislature, a right inestimable to them and formidable to tyrants only.

He has called together legislative bodies at places unusual, uncomfortable, and distant from the depository of their public records, for the sole purpose of fatiguing them into compliance with his measures.

He has dissolved Representative Houses repeatedly, for opposing with manly firmness his invasions on the rights of the people.

He has refused for a long time, after such dissolutions, to cause others to be elected; whereby the Legislative powers, incapable of Annihilation, have returned to the People at large for their exercise; the State remaining in the meantime exposed to all the dangers of invasion from without, and convulsions within.

He has endeavored to prevent the population of these States; for that purpose obstructing the Laws for Naturalization of Foreigners; refusing to pass others to encourage their migration hither, and raising the conditionsof new Appropriations of Lands.

He has obstructed the Administration of Justice, by refusing his Assent to Laws for establishing Judiciary powers.

He has made Judges dependent on his Will alone, for the tenure of their offices, and the amount and payment of their salaries.

He has erected a multitude of New Offices, and sent hither swarms of Officers to harass our people, and eat out their substance.

He has kept among us, in times of peace, Standing Armies without the consent of our legislatures.

He has affected to render the Military independent of and superior to Civil power.

He has combined with others to subject us to a jurisdiction foreign to our constitution, and unacknowledged by our laws; giving his Assent to their Acts of Pretended Legislation:

For Quartering large bodies of armed troops among us:

For protecting them, by a mock Trial, from punishment for any Murders which they should commit on the Inhabitants of these States:

For cutting off our Trade with all parts of the world:

For imposing Taxes on us without our consent:

For depriving us in many cases, of the benefits of Trial by Jury:

For transporting us beyond Seas to be tried for pretended offences

For abolishing the free System of English Laws in a neighboring Province, establishing therein an Arbitary government, and enlarging its Boundaries so as to render it at once an example and fit instrument for introducing the same absolute rule in these Colonies:

For taking away our Charters, abolishing our most valuable Laws, and altering fundamentally the Forms of our Governments:

For suspending our own Legislatures and declaring themselves invested with power to legislate for us in all cases whatsoever.

He has abdicated government here, by declaring us out of his Protection and waging War against us.

He has plundered our seas, ravaged our Coasts, burnt our towns, and destroyed the lives of our people.

He is at this time transporting large Armies of foreign Mercenaries to compleat the works of death, desolation and tyranny, already begun with circumstances of Cruelty & perfidy scarcely paralleled in the most barbarous ages, and totally unworthy of the Head of a civilized nation.

He has constrained our fellow Citizens taken Captive on the high Seas to bear Arms against their Country, to become the executioners of their friends and Brethren, or to fall themselves by their Hands.

He has excited domestic insurrections amongst us, and has endeavored to bring on the inhabitants of our frontiers, the merciless Indian savages, whose known rule of warfare, is undistinguished destruction of all ages, sexes and conditions.

In every stage of these Oppressions We have Petitioned for Redress in the most humble terms: Our repeated Petitions have been answered only by repeated injury. A Prince, whose character is thus marked by every act which may define a Tyrant, is unfit to be the ruler of a free people.

Nor have We been wanting in attention to our British brethren. We have warned them from time to time of attempts by their legislature to extend an unwarrantable jurisdiction over us. We have reminded them of the circumstances of our emigration and settlement here. We have appealed to their native justice and magnanimity, and we have conjured them by the ties of our common kindred to disavow these usurpations, which, would inevitably interrupt our connections and correspondence. They too have been deaf to the voice of justice and of consanguinity.

We must, therefore, acquiesce in the necessity, which denounces our Separation, and hold them, as we hold the rest of mankind, Enemies in War, in Peace Friends.

We, therefore, the Representatives of the united States of America, in General Congress, Assembled, appealing to the Supreme Judge of the world for the rectitude of our intentions, do, in the Name, and by the Authority of the good People of these Colonies, solemnly publish and declare, That these United Colonies are, and of Right ought to be Free and Independent States; that they are Absolved from all Allegiance to the British Crown, and that all political connection between them and the State of Great Britain, is and ought to be totally dissolved; and that as Free and Independent States, they have full Power to levy War, conclude Peace, contract Alliances, establish Commerce, and to do all other Acts and Things which independent States may of right do. And for the support of this Declaration, with a firm reliance on the protection of divine Providence, we mutually pledge to each other our Lives, our Fortunes and our sacred Honor.

The 56 signatures on the Declaration appear in the positions indicated:

Column 1
Georgia:
Button Gwinnett
Lyman Hall
George Walton

Column 2
North Carolina:
William Hooper
Joseph Hewes
John Penn

South Carolina:
Edward Rutledge
Thomas Heyward, Jr.
Thomas Lynch, Jr.
Arthur Middleton

Column 3
Massachusetts:
John Hancock

Maryland:
Samuel Chase
William Paca
Thomas Stone
Charles Carroll of Carrollton

Virginia:
George Wythe
Richard Henry Lee
Thomas Jefferson
Benjamin Harrison
Thomas Nelson, Jr.
Francis Lightfoot Lee
Carter Braxton

Column 4
Pennsylvania:
Robert Morris
Benjamin Rush
Benjamin Franklin
John Morton
George Clymer
James Smith
George Taylor
James Wilson
George Ross

Delaware:
Caesar Rodney
George Read
Thomas McKean

Column 5
New York:
William Floyd
Philip Livingston
Francis Lewis
Lewis Morris

New Jersey:
Richard Stockton
John Witherspoon
Francis Hopkinson
John Hart
Abraham Clark

Column 6
New Hampshire:
Josiah Bartlett
William Whipple

Massachusetts:
Samuel Adams
John Adams
Robert Treat Paine
Elbridge Gerry

Rhode Island:
Stephen Hopkins
William Ellery

Connecticut:
Roger Sherman
Samuel Huntington
William Williams
Oliver Wolcott

New Hampshire:
Matthew Thornton

Transcription of the 1789 Joint Resolution of Congress Proposing 12 Amendments to the U.S. Constitution

On September 25, 1789, the First Congress of the United States proposed 12 amendments to the Constitution. The 1789 Joint Resolution of Congress proposing the amendments is on display in the Rotunda in the National Archives Museum. Ten of the proposed 12 amendments were ratified by three-fourths of the state legislatures on December 15, 1791. The ratified Articles (Articles 3–12) constitute the first 10 amendments of the Constitution, or the U.S. Bill of Rights. Article 1 was never ratified. In 1992, 203 years after it was proposed, Article 2 was ratified as the 27th Amendment to the Constitution.

THE Conventions of a number of the States, having at the time of their adopting the Constitution, expressed a desire, in order to prevent misconstruction or abuse of its powers, that further declaratory and restrictive clauses should be added: And as extending the ground of public confidence in the Government, will best ensure the beneficent ends of its institution.

RESOLVED by the Senate and House of Representatives of the United States of America, in Congress assembled, two thirds of both Houses concurring, that the following

Articles be proposed to the Legislatures of the several States, as amendments to the Constitution of the United States, all, or any of which Articles, when ratified by three fourths of the said Legislatures, to be valid to all intents and purposes, as part of the said Constitution; viz.

ARTICLES in addition to, and Amendment of the Constitution of the United States of America, proposed by Congress, and ratified by the Legislatures of the several States, pursuant to the fifth Article of the original Constitution.

Article the first. After the first enumeration required by the first article of the Constitution, there shall be one Representative for every thirty thousand, until the number shall amount to one hundred, after which the proportion shall be so regulated by Congress, that there shall be not less than one hundred Representatives, nor less than one Representative for every forty thousand persons, until the number of Representatives shall amount to two hundred; after which the proportion shall be so regulated by Congress, that there shall not be less than two hundred Representatives, nor more than one Representative for every fifty thousand persons.

Article the second. No law, varying the compensation for the services of the Senators and Representatives, shall take effect, until an election of Representatives shall have intervened.

Article the third. Congress shall make no law respecting an establishment of religion, or prohibiting the free exercise thereof; or abridging the freedom of speech, or of the press; or the right of the people peaceably to assemble, and to petition the Government for a redress of grievances.

Article the fourth.A well regulated Militia, being necessary to the security of a free State, the right of the people to keep and bear Arms, shall not be infringed.

Article the fifth. No Soldier shall, in time of peace be quartered in any house, without the consent of the Owner, nor in time of war, but in a manner to be prescribed by law.

Article the sixth. The right of the people to be secure in their persons, houses, papers, and effects, against unreasonable searches and seizures, shall not be violated, and no Warrants shall issue, but upon probable cause, supported by Oath or affirmation, and particularly describing the place to be searched, and the persons or things to be seized.

Article the seventh. No person shall be held to answer for a capital, or otherwise infamous crime, unless on a presentment or indictment of a Grand Jury, except in cases arising in the land or naval forces, or in the Militia, when in actual service in time of War or public danger; nor shall any person be subject for the same offence to be twice put in jeopardy of life or limb; nor shall be compelled in any criminal case to be a witness against himself, nor be deprived of life, liberty, or property, without due process of law; nor shall private property be taken for public use, without just compensation.

Article the eighth. In all criminal prosecutions, the accused shall enjoy the right to a speedy and public trial, by an impartial jury of the State and district wherein the crime shall have been committed, which district shall have been previously ascertained by law, and to be informed of the nature and cause of the accusation; to be confronted with the witnesses against him; to have compulsory process for obtaining witnesses in his favor, and to have the Assistance of Counsel for his defense.

Article the ninth. In suits at common law, where the value in controversy shall exceed twenty dollars, the right of trial by jury shall be preserved, and no fact tried by a jury, shall be otherwise re-examined in any Court of the United States, than according to the rules of the common law.

Article the tenth. Excessive bail shall not be required, nor excessive fines imposed, nor cruel and unusual punishments inflicted.

Article the eleventh. The enumeration in the Constitution, of certain rights, shall not be construed to deny or disparage others retained by the people.

Article the twelfth. The powers not delegated to the United States by the Constitution, nor prohibited by it to the States, are reserved to the States respectively, or to the people.

ATTEST,
Frederick Augustus Muhlenberg, Speaker of the House of Representatives John Adams, Vice-President of the United States, and President of the Senate John Beckley clerk of the House of Representatives, Sam. A Otis, Secretary of the Senate

The U.S. Bill of Rights

The Preamble to The Bill of Rights

Congress of the United States
begun and held at the City of New-York, on Wednesday the fourth of March, one thousand seven hundred and eighty nine.

THE Conventions of a number of the States, having at the time of their adopting the Constitution, expressed a desire, in order to prevent misconstruction or abuse of its powers, that further declaratory and restrictive clauses should be added: And as extending the ground of public confidence in the Government, will best ensure the beneficent ends of its institution.

RESOLVED by the Senate and House of Representatives of the United States of America, in Congress assembled, two thirds of both Houses concurring, that the following Articles be proposed to the Legislatures of the several States, as amendments to the Constitution of the United States, all, or any of which Articles, when ratified by three fourths of the said Legislatures, to be valid to all intents and purposes, as part of the said Constitution; viz.

ARTICLES in addition to, and Amendment of the Constitution of the United States of America, proposed by

Congress, and ratified by the Legislatures of the several States, pursuant to the fifth Article of the original Constitution.

Note: The following text is a transcription of the first ten amendments to the Constitution in their original form. These amendments were ratified December 15, 1791, and form what is known as the **"Bill of Rights."**

Amendment I

Congress shall make no law respecting an establishment of religion, or prohibiting the free exercise thereof; or abridging the freedom of speech, or of the press; or the right of the people peaceably to assemble, and to petition the Government for a redress of grievances.

Amendment II

A well regulated Militia, being necessary to the security of a free State, the right of the people to keep and bear Arms, shall not be infringed.

Amendment III

No Soldier shall, in time of peace be quartered in any house, without the consent of the Owner, nor in time of war, but in a manner to be prescribed by law.

Amendment IV

The right of the people to be secure in their persons, houses, papers, and effects, against unreasonable searches and seizures, shall not be violated, and no Warrants shall issue, but upon probable cause, supported by Oath or affirmation, and particularly describing the place to be searched, and the persons or things to be seized.

Amendment V

No person shall be held to answer for a capital, or otherwise infamous crime, unless on a presentment or indictment of a Grand Jury, except in cases arising in the land or naval forces, or in the Militia, when in actual service in time of War or public danger; nor shall any person be subject for the same offence to be twice put in jeopardy of life or limb; nor shall be compelled in any criminal case to be a witness against himself, nor be deprived of life, liberty, or property, without due process of law; nor shall private property be taken for public use, without just compensation.

Amendment VI

In all criminal prosecutions, the accused shall enjoy the right to a speedy and public trial, by an impartial jury of the State and district wherein the crime shall have been committed, which district shall have been previously ascertained by law, and to be informed of the nature and cause of the accusation; to be confronted with the witnesses against him; to have compulsory process for obtaining witnesses in his favor, and to have the Assistance of Counsel for his defence.

Amendment VII

In Suits at common law, where the value in controversy shall exceed twenty dollars, the right of trial by jury shall be preserved, and no fact tried by a jury, shall be otherwise re-examined in any Court of the United States, than according to the rules of the common law.

Amendment VIII

Excessive bail shall not be required, nor excessive fines imposed, nor cruel and unusual punishments inflicted.

Amendment IX

The enumeration in the Constitution, of certain rights, shall not be construed to deny or disparage others retained by the people.

Amendment X

The powers not delegated to the United States by the Constitution, nor prohibited by it to the States, are reserved to the States respectively, or to the people.

Note: The capitalization and punctuation in this version is from the enrolled original of the Joint Resolution of Congress proposing the Bill of Rights, which is on permanent display in the Rotunda of the National Archives Building, Washington, D.C.

The Constitution of the United States: A Transcription

Note: The following text is a transcription of the Constitution as it was inscribed by Jacob Shallus on parchment (the document on display in the Rotunda at the National Archives Museum.) Items that are hyperlinked have since been amended or superseded. The authenticated text *of the Constitution can be found on the website of the Government Printing Office.*

We the People of the United States, in Order to form a more perfect Union, establish Justice, insure domestic Tranquility, provide for the common defense, promote the general Welfare, and secure the Blessings of Liberty to ourselves and our Posterity, do ordain and establish this Constitution for the United States of America.

Article. I.
Section. 1.

All legislative Powers herein granted shall be vested in a Congress of the United States, which shall consist of a Senate and House of Representatives.

Section. 2.

The House of Representatives shall be composed of Members chosen every second Year by the People of the several States, and the Electors in each State shall have the Qualifications requisite for Electors of the most numerous Branch of the State Legislature.

No Person shall be a Representative who shall not have attained to the Age of twenty five Years, and been seven Years a Citizen of the United States, and who shall not, when elected, be an Inhabitant of that State in which he shall be chosen.

Representatives and direct Taxes shall be apportioned among the several States which may be included within this Union, according to their respective Numbers, which shall be determined by adding to the whole Number of free Persons, including those bound to Service for a Term of Years, and excluding Indians not taxed, three fifths of all other Persons. The actual Enumeration shall be made within three Years after the first Meeting of the Congress of the United States, and within every subsequent Term of ten Years, in such Manner as they shall by Law direct. The Number of Representatives shall not exceed one for every thirty Thousand, but each State shall have at Least one Representative; and until such enumeration shall be made, the State of New Hampshire shall be entitled to chuse three, Massachusetts eight, Rhode-Island and Providence Plantations one, Connecticut five, New-York six, New Jersey four, Pennsylvania eight, Delaware one, Maryland six, Virginia ten, North Carolina five, South Carolina five, and Georgia three.

When vacancies happen in the Representation from any State, the Executive Authority thereof shall issue Writs of Election to fill such Vacancies.

The House of Representatives shall chuse their Speaker and other Officers; and shall have the sole Power of Impeachment.

Section. 3.

The Senate of the United States shall be composed of two Senators from each State, chosen by the Legislature thereof, for six Years; and each Senator shall have one Vote.

Immediately after they shall be assembled in Consequence of the first Election, they shall be divided as equally as may be into three Classes. The Seats of the Senators of the first Class shall be vacated at the Expiration of the second Year, of the second Class at the Expiration of the fourth Year, and of the third Class at the Expiration of the sixth Year, so that one third may be chosen every second Year; and if Vacancies happen by

Resignation, or otherwise, during the Recess of the Legislature of any State, the Executive thereof may make temporary Appointments until the next Meeting of the Legislature, which shall then fill such Vacancies.

No Person shall be a Senator who shall not have attained to the Age of thirty Years, and been nine Years a Citizen of the United States, and who shall not, when elected, be an Inhabitant of that State for which he shall be chosen.

The Vice President of the United States shall be President of the Senate, but shall have no Vote, unless they be equally divided.

The Senate shall chuse their other Officers, and also a President pro tempore, in the Absence of the Vice President, or when he shall exercise the Office of President of the United States.

The Senate shall have the sole Power to try all Impeachments. When sitting for that Purpose, they shall be on Oath or Affirmation. When the President of the United States is tried, the Chief Justice shall preside: And no Person shall be convicted without the Concurrence of two thirds of the Members present.

Judgment in Cases of Impeachment shall not extend further than to removal from Office, and disqualification to hold and enjoy any Office of honor, Trust or Profit under the United States: but the Party convicted shall nevertheless be liable and subject to Indictment, Trial, Judgment and Punishment, according to Law.

Section. 4.

The Times, Places and Manner of holding Elections for Senators and Representatives, shall be prescribed in each State by the Legislature thereof; but the Congress may at any time by Law make or alter such Regulations, except as to the Places of chusing Senators.

The Congress shall assemble at least once in every Year, and such Meeting shall be on the first Monday in December, unless they shall by Law appoint a different Day.

Section. 5.

Each House shall be the Judge of the Elections, Returns and Qualifications of its own Members, and a Majority of each shall constitute a Quorum to do Business; but a smaller Number may adjourn from day to day, and may be authorized to compel the Attendance of absent Members, in such Manner, and under such Penalties as each House may provide.

Each House may determine the Rules of its Proceedings, punish its Members for disorderly Behaviour, and, with the Concurrence of two thirds, expel a Member.

Each House shall keep a Journal of its Proceedings, and from time to time publish the same, excepting such Parts as may in their Judgment require Secrecy; and the Yeas and Nays of the Members of either House on any question shall, at the Desire of one fifth of those Present, be entered on the Journal.

Neither House, during the Session of Congress, shall, without the Consent of the other, adjourn for more than three days, nor to any other Place than that in which the two Houses shall be sitting.

Section. 6.

The Senators and Representatives shall receive a Compensation for their Services, to be ascertained by Law, and paid out of the Treasury of the United States. They shall in all Cases, except Treason, Felony and Breach of the Peace, be privileged from Arrest during their Attendance at the Session of their respective Houses, and in going to and returning from the same; and for any Speech or Debate in either House, they shall not be questioned in any other Place.

No Senator or Representative shall, during the Time for which he was elected, be appointed to any civil Office under the Authority of the United States, which shall have been created, or the Emoluments whereof shall have been encreased during such time; and no Person holding any Office under the United States, shall be a Member of either House during his Continuance in Office.

Section. 7.

All Bills for raising Revenue shall originate in the House of Representatives; but the Senate may propose or concur with Amendments as on other Bills.

Every Bill which shall have passed the House of Representatives and the Senate, shall, before it become a Law, be presented to the President of the United States; If he approve he shall sign it, but if not he shall return it, with his Objections to that House in which it shall have originated, who shall enter the Objections at large on their Journal, and proceed to reconsider it. If after such Reconsideration two thirds of that House shall agree to pass the Bill, it shall be sent, together with the Objections, to the other House, by which it shall likewise be reconsidered, and if approved by two thirds of that House, it shall become a Law. But in all such Cases the Votes of both Houses shall be determined by yeas and Nays, and the Names of the Persons voting for and against the Bill shall be entered on the Journal of each House respectively. If any Bill shall not be returned by the President within ten Days (Sundays excepted) after it shall have been presented to him, the Same shall be a Law, in like Manner as if he had signed it, unless the Congress by their Adjournment prevent its Return, in which Case it shall not be a Law.

Every Order, Resolution, or Vote to which the Concurrence of the Senate and House of Representatives may be necessary (except on a question of Adjournment) shall be presented to the President of the United States; and before the Same shall take Effect, shall be approved by him, or being disapproved by him, shall be repassed by two thirds of the Senate and House of Representatives, according to the Rules and Limitations prescribed in the Case of a Bill.

Section. 8.

The Congress shall have Power To lay and collect Taxes, Duties, Imposts and Excises, to pay the Debts and provide for the common Defence and general Welfare of the United States; but all Duties, Imposts and Excises shall be uniform throughout the United States;

To borrow Money on the credit of the United States;

To regulate Commerce with foreign Nations, and among the several States, and with the Indian Tribes;

To establish an uniform Rule of Naturalization, and uniform Laws on the subject of Bankruptcies throughout the United States;

To coin Money, regulate the Value thereof, and of foreign Coin, and fix the Standard of Weights and Measures;

To provide for the Punishment of counterfeiting the Securities and current Coin of the United States;

To establish Post Offices and post Roads;

To promote the Progress of Science and useful Arts, by securing for limited Times to Authors and Inventors the exclusive Right to their respective Writings and Discoveries;

To constitute Tribunals inferior to the supreme Court;

To define and punish Piracies and Felonies committed on the high Seas, and Offences against the Law of Nations;

To declare War, grant Letters of Marque and Reprisal, and make Rules concerning Captures on Land and Water;

To raise and support Armies, but no Appropriation of Money to that Use shall be for a longer Term than two Years;

To provide and maintain a Navy;

To make Rules for the Government and Regulation of the land and naval Forces;

To provide for calling forth the Militia to execute the Laws of the Union, suppress Insurrections and repel Invasions;

To provide for organizing, arming, and disciplining, the Militia, and for governing such Part of them as may be employed in the Service of the United States, reserving to the States respectively, the Appointment of the Officers, and the Authority of training the Militia according to the discipline prescribed by Congress;

To exercise exclusive Legislation in all Cases whatsoever, over such District (not exceeding ten Miles square) as may, by Cession of particular States, and the Acceptance of Congress, become the Seat of the Government of the United States, and to exercise like Authority over all Places purchased by the Consent of the Legislature of the State in which the Same shall be, for the Erection of Forts, Magazines, Arsenals, dock-Yards, and other needful Buildings;—And

To make all Laws which shall be necessary and proper for carrying into Execution the foregoing Powers, and all other Powers vested by this Constitution in the Government of the United States, or in any Department or Officer thereof.

Section 9.

The Migration or Importation of such Persons as any of the States now existing shall think proper to admit, shall not be prohibited by the Congress prior to the Year one thousand eight hundred and eight, but a Tax or duty may be imposed on such Importation, not exceeding ten dollars for each Person.

The Privilege of the Writ of Habeas Corpus shall not be suspended, unless when in Cases of Rebellion or Invasion the public Safety may require it.

No Bill of Attainder or ex post facto Law shall be passed.

No Capitation, or other direct, Tax shall be laid, unless in Proportion to the Census or enumeration herein before directed to be taken.

No Tax or Duty shall be laid on Articles exported from any State. No Preference shall be given by any Regulation of Commerce or Revenue to the Ports of one State over those of another: nor shall Vessels bound to, or from, one State, be obliged to enter, clear, or pay Duties in another.

No Money shall be drawn from the Treasury, but in Consequence of Appropriations made by Law; and a regular Statement and Account of the Receipts and Expenditures of all public Money shall be published from time to time.

No Title of Nobility shall be granted by the United States: And no Person holding any Office of Profit or Trust under them, shall, without the Consent of the Congress, accept of any present, Emolument, Office, or Title, of any kind whatever, from any King, Prince, or foreign State.

Section. 10.

No State shall enter into any Treaty, Alliance, or Confederation; grant Letters of Marque and Reprisal; coin Money; emit Bills of Credit; make any Thing but gold and silver Coin a Tender in Payment of Debts; pass any Bill of Attainder, ex post facto Law, or Law impairing the Obligation of Contracts, or grant any Title of Nobility.

No State shall, without the Consent of the Congress, lay any Imposts or Duties on Imports or Exports, except what may be absolutely necessary for executing it's inspection Laws: and the net Produce of all Duties and Imposts, laid by any State on Imports or Exports, shall be for the Use of the Treasury of the United States; and all such Laws shall be subject to the Revision and Controul of the Congress.

No State shall, without the Consent of Congress, lay any Duty of Tonnage, keep Troops, or Ships of War in time of Peace, enter into any Agreement or Compact with another State, or with a foreign Power, or engage in War, unless actually invaded, or in such imminent Danger as will not admit of delay.

Article. II.

Section. 1.

The executive Power shall be vested in a President of the United States of America. He shall hold his Office during the Term of four Years, and, together with the Vice President, chosen for the same Term, be elected, as follows

Each State shall appoint, in such Manner as the Legislature thereof may direct, a Number of Electors, equal to the whole Number of Senators and Representatives to which the State may be entitled in the Congress: but no Senator or Representative, or Person holding an Office of Trust or Profit under the United States, shall be appointed an Elector.

The Electors shall meet in their respective States, and vote by Ballot for two Persons, of whom one at least shall not be an Inhabitant of the same State with themselves. And they shall make a List of all the Persons voted for, and of the Number of Votes for each; which List they shall sign and certify, and transmit sealed to the Seat of the Government of the United States, directed to the President of the Senate. The President of the Senate shall, in the Presence of the Senate and House of Representatives, open all the Certificates, and the Votes shall then be counted. The Person having the greatest Number of Votes shall be the President, if such Number be a Majority of the whole Number of Electors appointed; and if there be more than one who have such Majority, and have an equal Number of Votes, then the House of Representatives shall immediately chuse by Ballot one of them for President; and if no Person have a Majority, then from the five highest on the List the said House shall in like Manner chuse the President. But in chusing the President, the Votes shall be taken by States, the Representation from each State having one Vote; A quorum for this Purpose shall consist of a Member or Members from two thirds of the States, and a Majority of all the States shall be necessary to a Choice. In every Case, after the Choice of the President, the Person having the greatest Number of Votes of the Electors shall be the Vice President. But if there should remain two or more who have equal Votes, the Senate shall chuse from them by Ballot the Vice President.

The Congress may determine the Time of chusing the Electors, and the Day on which they shall give their Votes; which Day shall be the same throughout the United States.

No Person except a natural born Citizen, or a Citizen of the United States, at the time of the Adoption of this Constitution, shall be eligible to the Office of President; neither shall any Person be eligible to that Office who shall not have attained to the Age of thirty five Years, and been fourteen Years a Resident within the United States.

In Case of the Removal of the President from Office, or of his Death, Resignation, or Inability to discharge the Powers and Duties of the said Office, the Same shall devolve on the Vice President, and the Congress may by Law provide for the Case of Removal, Death, Resignation or Inability, both of the President and Vice President, declaring what Officer shall then act as President, and such Officer shall act accordingly, until the Disability be removed, or a President shall be elected.

The President shall, at stated Times, receive for his Services, a Compensation, which shall neither be encreased nor diminished during the Period for which he shall have been elected, and he shall not receive within that Period any other Emolument from the United States, or any of them.

Before he enter on the Execution of his Office, he shall take the following Oath or Affirmation:—"I do solemnly swear (or affirm) that I will faithfully execute the Office of President of the United States, and will to the best of my Ability, preserve, protect and defend the Constitution of the United States."

Section. 2.

The President shall be Commander in Chief of the Army and Navy of the United States, and of the Militia of the several States, when called into the actual Service of the United States; he may require the Opinion, in writing, of the principal Officer in each of the executive Departments, upon any Subject relating to the Duties of their respective Offices, and he shall have Power to grant Reprieves and Pardons for Offences against the United States, except in Cases of Impeachment.

He shall have Power, by and with the Advice and Consent of the Senate, to make Treaties, provided two thirds of the Senators present concur; and he shall nominate, and by and with the Advice and Consent of the Senate, shall appoint Ambassadors, other public Ministers and Consuls,

Judges of the supreme Court, and all other Officers of the United States, whose Appointments are not herein otherwise provided for, and which shall be established by Law: but the Congress may by Law vest the Appointment of such inferior Officers, as they think proper, in the President alone, in the Courts of Law, or in the Heads of Departments.

The President shall have Power to fill up all Vacancies that may happen during the Recess of the Senate, by granting Commissions which shall expire at the End of their next Session.

Section. 3.

He shall from time to time give to the Congress Information of the State of the Union, and recommend to their Consideration such Measures as he shall judge necessary and expedient; he may, on extraordinary Occasions, convene both Houses, or either of them, and in Case of Disagreement between them, with Respect to the Time of Adjournment, he may adjourn them to such Time as he shall think proper; he shall receive Ambassadors and other public Ministers; he shall take Care that the Laws be faithfully executed, and shall Commission all the Officers of the United States.

Section. 4.

The President, Vice President and all civil Officers of the United States, shall be removed from Office on Impeachment for, and Conviction of, Treason, Bribery, or other high Crimes and Misdemeanors.

Article III.

Section. 1.

The judicial Power of the United States, shall be vested in one supreme Court, and in such inferior Courts as the Congress may from time to time ordain and establish. The Judges, both of the supreme and inferior Courts, shall hold their Offices during good Behaviour, and shall, at stated Times, receive for their Services, a Compensation, which shall not be diminished during their Continuance in Office.

Section. 2.

The judicial Power shall extend to all Cases, in Law and Equity, arising under this Constitution, the Laws of the United States, and Treaties made, or which shall be made, under their Authority;—to all Cases affecting Ambassadors, other public Ministers and Consuls;—to all Cases of admiralty and maritime Jurisdiction;—to Controversies to which the United States shall be a Party;—to Controversies between two or more States;—between a State and Citizens of another State,—between

Citizens of different States,—between Citizens of the same State claiming Lands under Grants of different States, and between a State, or the Citizens thereof, and foreign States, Citizens or Subjects.

In all Cases affecting Ambassadors, other public Ministers and Consuls, and those in which a State shall be Party, the supreme Court shall have original Jurisdiction. In all the other Cases before mentioned, the supreme Court shall have appellate Jurisdiction, both as to Law and Fact, with such Exceptions, and under such Regulations as the Congress shall make.

The Trial of all Crimes, except in Cases of Impeachment, shall be by Jury; and such Trial shall be held in the State where the said Crimes shall have been committed; but when not committed within any State, the Trial shall be at such Place or Places as the Congress may by Law have directed.

Section. 3.

Treason against the United States, shall consist only in levying War against them, or in adhering to their Enemies, giving them Aid and Comfort. No Person shall be convicted of Treason unless on the Testimony of two Witnesses to the same overt Act, or on Confession in open Court.

The Congress shall have Power to declare the Punishment of Treason, but no Attainder of Treason shall work Corruption of Blood, or Forfeiture except during the Life of the Person attainted.

Article IV.

Section. 1.

Full Faith and Credit shall be given in each State to the public Acts, Records, and judicial Proceedings of every other State. And the Congress may by general Laws prescribe the Manner in which such Acts, Records and Proceedings shall be proved, and the Effect thereof.

Section. 2.

The Citizens of each State shall be entitled to all Privileges and Immunities of Citizens in the several States.

A Person charged in any State with Treason, Felony, or other Crime, who shall flee from Justice, and be found in another State, shall on Demand of the executive Authority of the State from which he fled, be delivered up, to be removed to the State having Jurisdiction of the Crime.

No Person held to Service or Labour in one State, under the Laws thereof, escaping into another, shall, in Consequence of any Law or Regulation therein, be discharged from such Service or Labour, but shall be delivered up on Claim of the Party to whom such Service or Labour may be due.

Section. 3.

New States may be admitted by the Congress into this Union; but no new State shall be formed or erected within the Jurisdiction of any other State; nor any State be formed by the Junction of two or more States, or Parts of States, without the Consent of the Legislatures of the States concerned as well as of the Congress.

The Congress shall have Power to dispose of and make all needful Rules and Regulations respecting the Territory or other Property belonging to the United States; and nothing in this Constitution shall be so construed as to Prejudice any Claims of the United States, or of any particular State.

Section. 4.

The United States shall guarantee to every State in this Union a Republican Form of Government, and shall protect each of them against Invasion; and on Application of the Legislature, or of the Executive (when the Legislature cannot be convened), against domestic Violence.

Article. V.

The Congress, whenever two thirds of both Houses shall deem it necessary, shall propose Amendments to this Constitution, or, on the Application of the Legislatures of two thirds of the several States, shall call a Convention for proposing Amendments, which, in either Case, shall be valid to all Intents and Purposes, as Part of this Constitution, when ratified by the Legislatures of three fourths of the several States, or by Conventions in three fourths thereof, as the one or the other Mode of Ratification may be proposed by the Congress; Provided that no Amendment which may be made prior to the Year One thousand eight hundred and eight shall in any Manner affect the first and fourth Clauses in the Ninth Section of the first Article; and that no State, without its Consent, shall be deprived of its equal Suffrage in the Senate.

Article. VI.

All Debts contracted and Engagements entered into, before the Adoption of this Constitution, shall be as valid against the United States under this Constitution, as under the Confederation.

This Constitution, and the Laws of the United States which shall be made in Pursuance thereof; and all Treaties made, or which shall be made, under the Authority of the United States, shall be the supreme Law of the Land; and the Judges in every State shall be bound thereby, any Thing in the Constitution or Laws of any State to the Contrary notwithstanding.

The Senators and Representatives before mentioned, and the Members of the several State Legislatures, and all executive and judicial Officers, both of the United States and of the several States, shall be bound by Oath or Affirmation, to support this Constitution; but no religious Test shall ever be required as a Qualification to any Office or public Trust under the United States.

Article. VII.

The Ratification of the Conventions of nine States, shall be sufficient for the Establishment of this Constitution between the States so ratifying the Same.

The Word, "the," being interlined between the seventh and eighth Lines of the first Page, The Word "Thirty" being partly written on an Erazure in the fifteenth Line of the first Page, The Words "is tried" being interlined between the thirty second and thirty third Lines of the first Page and the Word "the" being interlined between the forty third and forty fourth Lines of the second Page.

Attest William Jackson Secretary done in Convention by the Unanimous Consent of the States present the Seventeenth Day of September in the Year of our Lord one thousand seven hundred and Eighty seven and of the Independance of the United States of America the Twelfth In witness whereof We have hereunto subscribed our Names,

G. Washington
Presidt and deputy from Virginia

Delaware
Geo: Read
Gunning Bedford jun
John Dickinson
Richard Bassett
Jaco: Broom

Maryland
James McHenry
Dan of St Thos. Jenifer
Danl. Carroll

Virginia
John Blair
James Madison Jr.

North Carolina
Wm. Blount
Richd. Dobbs Spaight
Hu Williamson

South Carolina
J. Rutledge
Charles Cotesworth Pinckney
Charles Pinckney
Pierce Butler

Georgia
William Few
Abr Baldwin

New Hampshire
John Langdon
Nicholas Gilman

Massachusetts
Nathaniel Gorham
Rufus King

Connecticut
Wm. Saml. Johnson
Roger Sherman

New York
Alexander Hamilton

New Jersey
Wil: Livingston
David Brearley
Wm. Paterson
Jona: Dayton

Pensylvania
B Franklin
Thomas Mifflin
Robt. Morris
Geo. Clymer
Thos. FitzSimons
Jared Ingersoll
James Wilson
Gouv Morris

The Constitution: Amendments 11-27

AMENDMENT XI - Passed by Congress March 4, 1794. Ratified February 7, 1795.
Note: Article III, section 2, of the Constitution was modified by amendment 11.
The Judicial power of the United States shall not be construed to extend to any suit in law or equity, commenced or prosecuted against one of the United States by Citizens of another State, or by Citizens or Subjects of any Foreign State.

AMENDMENT XII - Passed by Congress December 9, 1803. Ratified June 15, 1804.
Note: A portion of Article II, section 1 of the Constitution was superseded by the 12th amendment.
The Electors shall meet in their respective states and vote by ballot for President and Vice-President, one of whom, at least, shall not be an inhabitant of the same state with themselves; they shall name in their ballots the person voted for as President, and in distinct ballots the person voted for as Vice-President, and they shall make distinct lists of all persons voted for as President, and of all persons voted for as Vice-President, and of the number of votes for each, which lists they shall sign and certify, and transmit sealed to the seat of the government of the

United States, directed to the President of the Senate; -- the President of the Senate shall, in the presence of the Senate and House of Representatives, open all the certificates and the votes shall then be counted; -- The person having the greatest number of votes for President, shall be the President, if such number be a majority of the whole number of Electors appointed; and if no person have such majority, then from the persons having the highest numbers not exceeding three on the list of those voted for as President, the House of Representatives shall choose immediately, by ballot, the President. But in choosing the President, the votes shall be taken by states, the representation from each state having one vote; a quorum for this purpose shall consist of a member or members from two-thirds of the states, and a majority of all the states shall be necessary to a choice. [And if the House of Representatives shall not choose a President whenever the right of choice shall devolve upon them, before the fourth day of March next following, then the Vice-President shall act as President, as in case of the death or other constitutional disability of the President.]* The person having the greatest number of votes as Vice-President, shall be the Vice-President, if such number be a majority of the whole number of Electors appointed, and if no person have a majority, then from the two highest numbers on the list, the Senate shall choose the Vice-President; a quorum for the purpose shall consist of two-thirds of the whole number of Senators, and a majority of the whole number shall be necessary to a choice. But no person constitutionally ineligible to the office of President shall be eligible to that of Vice-President of the United States.

Superseded by section 3 of the 20th amendment.

AMENDMENT XIII - Passed by Congress January 31, 1865. Ratified December 6, 1865.
Note: A portion of Article IV, section 2, of the Constitution was superseded by the 13th amendment.

Section 1.Neither slavery nor involuntary servitude, except as a punishment for crime whereof the party shall have been duly convicted, shall exist within the United States, or any place subject to their jurisdiction.

Section 2.Congress shall have power to enforce this article by appropriate legislation.

AMENDMENT XIV - Passed by Congress June 13, 1866. Ratified July 9, 1868.
Note: Article I, section 2, of the Constitution was modified by section 2 of the 14th amendment.
Section 1.All persons born or naturalized in the United States, and subject to the jurisdiction thereof, are citizens of the United States and of the State wherein they reside.

No State shall make or enforce any law which shall abridge the privileges or immunities of citizens of the United States; nor shall any State deprive any person of life, liberty, or property, without due process of law; nor deny to any person within its jurisdiction the equal protection of the laws.

Section 2. Representatives shall be apportioned among the several States according to their respective numbers, counting the whole number of persons in each State, excluding Indians not taxed. But when the right to vote at any election for the choice of electors for President and Vice-President of the United States, Representatives in Congress, the Executive and Judicial officers of a State, or the members of the Legislature thereof, is denied to any of the male inhabitants of such State, being twenty-one years of age,* and citizens of the United States, or in any way abridged, except for participation in rebellion, or other crime, the basis of representation therein shall be reduced in the proportion which the number of such male citizens shall bear to the whole number of male citizens twenty-one years of age in such State.

Section 3. No person shall be a Senator or Representative in Congress, or elector of President and Vice-President, or hold any office, civil or military, under the United States, or under any State, who, having previously taken an oath, as a member of Congress, or as an officer of the United States, or as a member of any State legislature, or as an executive or judicial officer of any State, to support the Constitution of the United States, shall have engaged in insurrection or rebellion against the same, or given aid or comfort to the enemies thereof. But Congress may by a vote of two-thirds of each House, remove such disability.

Section 4.The validity of the public debt of the United States, authorized by law, including debts incurred for payment of pensions and bounties for services in suppressing insurrection or rebellion, shall not be questioned. But neither the United States nor any State shall assume or pay any debt or obligation incurred in aid of insurrection or rebellion against the United States, or any claim for the loss or emancipation of any slave; but all such debts, obligations and claims shall be held illegal and void.

Section 5.
The Congress shall have the power to enforce, by appropriate legislation, the provisions of this article.
Changed by section 1 of the 26th amendment.

AMENDMENT XV - Passed by Congress February 26, 1869. Ratified February 3, 1870.

Section 1. The right of citizens of the United States to vote shall not be denied or abridged by the United States or by any State on account of race, color, or previous condition of servitude.

Section 2. The Congress shall have the power to enforce this article by appropriate legislation.

AMENDMENT XVI - Passed by Congress July 2, 1909. Ratified February 3, 1913.
Note: Article I, section 9, of the Constitution was modified by amendment 16.

The Congress shall have power to lay and collect taxes on incomes, from whatever source derived, without apportionment among the several States, and without regard to any census or enumeration.

AMENDMENT XVII - Passed by Congress May 13, 1912. Ratified April 8, 1913

Note: Article I, section 3, of the Constitution was modified by the 17th amendment.

The Senate of the United States shall be composed of two Senators from each State, elected by the people thereof, for six years; and each Senator shall have one vote. The electors in each State shall have the qualifications requisite for electors of the most numerous branch of the State legislatures.

When vacancies happen in the representation of any State in the Senate, the executive authority of such State shall issue writs of election to fill such vacancies: Provided, That the legislature of any State may empower the executive thereof to make temporary appointments until the people fill the vacancies by election as the legislature may direct.

This amendment shall not be so construed as to affect the election or term of any Senator chosen before it becomes valid as part of the Constitution.

AMENDMENT XVIII - Passed by Congress December 18, 1917. Ratified January 16, 1919. Repealed by amendment 21.

Section 1.After one year from the ratification of this article the manufacture, sale, or transportation of intoxicating liquors within, the importation thereof into, or the exportation thereof from the United States and all territory subject to the jurisdiction thereof for beverage purposes is hereby prohibited.

Section 2.The Congress and the several States shall have concurrent power to enforce this article by appropriate legislation.

Section 3. This article shall be inoperative unless it shall have been ratified as an amendment to the Constitution by the legislatures of the several States, as provided in the Constitution, within seven years from the date of the submission hereof to the States by the Congress.

AMENDMENT XIX - Passed by Congress June 4, 1919. Ratified August 18, 1920.

The right of citizens of the United States to vote shall not be denied or abridged by the United States or by any State on account of sex.

Congress shall have power to enforce this article by appropriate legislation.

AMENDMENT XX - Passed by Congress March 2, 1932. Ratified January 23, 1933.

Note: Article I, section 4, of the Constitution was modified by section 2 of this amendment. In addition, a portion of the 12th amendment was superseded by section 3.

Section 1. The terms of the President and the Vice President shall end at noon on the 20th day of January, and the terms of Senators and Representatives at noon on the 3d day of January, of the years in which such terms would have ended if this article had not been ratified; and the terms of their successors shall then begin.

Section 2. The Congress shall assemble at least once in every year, and such meeting shall begin at noon on the 3d day of January, unless they shall by law appoint a different day.

Section 3. If, at the time fixed for the beginning of the term of the President, the President elect shall have died, the Vice President elect shall become President. If a President shall not have been chosen before the time fixed for the beginning of his term, or if the President elect shall have failed to qualify, then the Vice President elect shall act as President until a President shall have qualified; and the Congress may by law provide for the case wherein neither a President elect nor a Vice President shall have qualified, declaring who shall then act as President, or the manner in which one who is to act shall be selected, and such person shall act accordingly until a President or Vice President shall have qualified.

Section 4. The Congress may by law provide for the case of the death of any of the persons from whom the House of Representatives may choose a President whenever the right of choice shall have devolved upon them, and for the case of the death of any of the persons from whom the Senate may choose a Vice President whenever the right of choice shall have devolved upon them.

Section 5.Sections 1 and 2 shall take effect on the 15th day of October following the ratification of this article.

Section 6.This article shall be inoperative unless it shall have been ratified as an amendment to the Constitution by the legislatures of three-fourths of the several States within seven years from the date of its submission.

AMENDMENT XXI - Passed by Congress February 20, 1933. Ratified December 5, 1933.

Section 1.The eighteenth article of amendment to the Constitution of the United States is hereby repealed.

Section 2.The transportation or importation into any State, Territory, or Possession of the United States for delivery or use therein of intoxicating liquors, in violation of the laws thereof, is hereby prohibited.
Section 3.This article shall be inoperative unless it shall have been ratified as an amendment to the Constitution by conventions in the several States, as provided in the Constitution, within seven years from the date of the submission hereof to the States by the Congress.

AMENDMENT XXII - Passed by Congress March 21, 1947. Ratified February 27, 1951.

Section 1.No person shall be elected to the office of the President more than twice, and no person who has held the office of President, or acted as President, for more than two years of a term to which some other person was elected President shall be elected to the office of President more than once. But this Article shall not apply to any person holding the office of President when this Article was proposed by Congress, and shall not prevent any person who may be holding the office of President, or acting as President, during the term within which this Article becomes operative from holding the office of President or acting as President during the remainder of such term.

Section 2.This article shall be inoperative unless it shall have been ratified as an amendment to the Constitution by the legislatures of three-fourths of the several States within seven years from the date of its submission to the States by the Congress.

AMENDMENT XXIII - Passed by Congress June 16, 1960. Ratified March 29, 1961.

Section 1.The District constituting the seat of Government of the United States shall appoint in such manner as Congress may direct: A number of electors of President and Vice President equal to the whole number of Senators and Representatives in Congress to which the District would be entitled if it were a State, but in no event more than the least populous State; they shall be in addition to those appointed by the States, but they shall be considered, for the purposes of the election of President and Vice President, to be electors appointed by a State; and they shall meet in the District and perform such duties as provided by the twelfth article of amendment.

Section 2. The Congress shall have power to enforce this article by appropriate legislation.

AMENDMENT XXIV - Passed by Congress August 27, 1962. Ratified January 23, 1964.

Section 1. The right of citizens of the United States to vote in any primary or other election for President or Vice President, for electors for President or Vice President, or for Senator or Representative in Congress, shall not be denied or abridged by the United States or any State by reason of failure to pay poll tax or other tax.

Section 2. The Congress shall have power to enforce this article by appropriate legislation.

AMENDMENT XXV - Passed by Congress July 6, 1965. Ratified February 10, 1967.

Note: Article II, section 1, of the Constitution was affected by the 25th amendment.

Section 1. In case of the removal of the President from office or of his death or resignation, the Vice President shall become President.

Section 2. Whenever there is a vacancy in the office of the Vice President the President shall nominate a Vice President who shall take office upon confirmation by a majority vote of both Houses of Congress.

Section 3. Whenever the President transmits to the President pro tempore of the Senate and the Speaker of the House of Representatives his written declaration that he is unable to discharge the powers and duties of his office, and until he transmits to them a written declaration to the contrary, such powers and duties shall be discharged by the Vice President as Acting President.

Section 4. Whenever the Vice President and a majority of either the principal officers of the executive departments or of such other body as Congress may by law provide, transmit to the President pro tempore of the Senate and the Speaker of the House of Representatives their written declaration that the President is unable to discharge the powers and duties of his office, the Vice President shall immediately assume the powers and duties of the office as Acting President. Thereafter, when the President transmits to the President pro tempore of the Senate and the Speaker of the House of Representatives his written declaration that no inability exists, he shall resume the powers and duties of his office unless the Vice President and a majority of either the principal officers of the executive department or of such other body as Congress may by law provide, transmit within four days to the President pro tempore of the Senate and the Speaker of the House of Representatives their written declaration that the President is unable to discharge the powers and duties of his office. Thereupon Congress shall decide the issue, assembling within forty-eight hours for that purpose if not in session. If the Congress, within twenty-one days after receipt of the latter written declaration, or, if Congress is not in session, within twenty-one days after Congress is required to assemble, determines by two-thirds vote of both Houses that the President is unable to discharge the powers and duties of his office, the Vice President shall continue to discharge the same as Acting President; otherwise, the President shall resume the powers and duties of his office.

AMENDMENT XXVI - Passed by Congress March 23, 1971. Ratified July 1, 1971.

Note: Amendment 14, section 2, of the Constitution was modified by section 1 of the 26th amendment.

Section 1.The right of citizens of the United States, who are eighteen years of age or older, to vote shall not be denied or abridged by the United States or by any State on account of age.

Section 2.The Congress shall have power to enforce this article by appropriate legislation.

AMENDMENT XXVII - Originally proposed Sept. 25, 1789. Ratified May 7, 1992.

No law, varying the compensation for the services of the Senators and Representatives, shall take effect, until an election of representatives shall have intervened.

Part 2: Blog Articles from *Our Caravan*

Each essay included in Part 2 was written in search of a resolution through Reaction, Research and Expression.

Reaction was usually visceral and was largely based on what I heard, saw or read.

Research helped me to better understand why I reacted and that often led me toward a much needed personal expression.

Expression, the essay itself, finally led me to personal resolution. In searching, I became more certain of what I believed and why.

All that remained for me was to share my perception of the newly discovered piece of the map with others.

I am comfortable knowing some of you will agree with my thoughts and some of you will not.

It is in your personal understanding of why you agree or disagree and your own resolution of what and why you believe something that is most important to me.

Plato recognized *"The beginning is the most important part of any work."*

Enjoy your journey.

The "We the People" Map

I remember when we knew and understood safety and trust and how it felt. We were proud. We believed we were unique and we believed that if we followed our maps all problems could and would be solved. Today, we seem to be losing those maps piece by piece. We are also losing our national sense of purpose and direction "We" is repeated often in this article because "We" are the current descendants of the people speaking in the preamble to the Constitution of the United States. The events "We" view in today's Washington are, therefore, even more frightening. The recent words and images of Washington and our nation's media present us as a country reduced to a war of words, name calling, labeling, posturing, clear ignorance of the Constitution and even lies by the President. These images provide the "We the people" a troubling slide show of a very rapidly changing constitutional map and a potentially bleak future

"We the People of the United States, in Order to form a more perfect Union, establish Justice, insure domestic Tranquility, provide for the common defense, promote the general Welfare, and secure the Blessings of Liberty to ourselves and our Posterity, do ordain and establish this Constitution for the United States of America."

The Bill of Rights were created and added to these historic words to prevent a "misconstruction or abuse of constitutional powers." These ten "unalienable" rights additionally increased the people's confidence in the government which the Framers had created.

"Then" and "Now" comparisons have been used to present two different pictures of "We the People". The words above remain the same today but their original meanings and their promises are being challenged.

Then: Our Framers specifically chose to execute a limited Executive, Legislative and Judicial government. The creation of the Bill of Rights made it complete with specific checks and balances and limitations for each branch and very specific rights granted to the states and to the people.

Now: Our government grows larger and larger with each passing day. "We the People" are increasingly cared for much as a good farmer tends to his livestock. The steady stream of additional new rules and mandates increasingly handicap prior guaranteed states rights and states have little or no choice except to bow to an ever demanding *big government can do it better and a you are not as intelligent as us philosophy*

Then: Our Founders were either Federalist or Non Federalist. The Non Federalists openly feared a centralized and powerful government. To reduce Non Federalists fears, our first senators, were elected by state legislatures rather than by a direct citizen vote. Those state senators served at the pleasure of the state and not the government. They were expected to faithfully represent state desires and not their own or the desires of others. Centralized power was, indeed, limited by specific checks.

Now: The 17th Amendment to the Constitution was passed by Congress on May 13, 1912 and Ratified on April 8, 1913. It was here that we destroyed the Framers intent. Some senators clearly do not even try to protect the states from the government and they all seem to seek continued status in its chambers. States' rights are clearly being limited and, our government has now grown to those levels feared and rejected by the Non Federalists.

Then: The focus of the Supreme Court was specifically limited to "all Cases in Law and Equity, arising under this Constitution". The Court's Justices had identified and limited responsibilities.

Now: Today's judges experience lifelong appointments and appear to function well beyond their intended purposes. At great risk to themselves and us, they have chosen not to be limited to decisions to "support" and "protect" the Constitution. They now create new laws.

The "Then" and "Now " guide above also reveals the presence of increased citizens, elected leaders and judges all claiming our Constitution and Bill of Rights are quaint and antiquated at best and are not representative or workable today. These individuals propose and support the adoption of different beliefs and values. We must learn to understand them as Progressives.

By carefully reading and considering well established progressive goals and their proclaimed benchmark achievements from President Woodrow Wilson through the last 100 plus years to Barack Obama you will self discover a planned piece by piece constitutional republic versus a utopian values struggle. Unlike our Founders secure and clear path, the utopian path is very steep, slippery and dangerous and *it has always failed*.

It is, of course, possible that we may someday experience the emergence of another Founder's type leader and the return to what "We" once understood a life time ago.

In this spirit, I end here and offer the words of Walt Kelly's cartoon character, "Pogo": **"Sir, we have met the enemy and he is us."**

Liberty Is Our Most Important Word

I have grown increasingly uncomfortable because of the dangerous places that our nation's progressive elected leaders are taking this nation. I could avoid these concerns by saying and doing nothing or simply stating to others that I am only one person and can do nothing to prevent what is happening. However, the words of Martin Luther King keep blocking any and all possible paths leading to an escape from my personal responsibilities. He said: "Our lives begin to end the day we become silent about things that matter." I choose, therefore, to share some "Things That Matter" for your consideration.

Without question, The Declaration of Independence, The Constitution of the United States, the Bill of Rights and Amendments numbered 11 through 27 all matter.

Can you name a commonly overlooked word carrying the weight and promise of vast historical and personal importance that also matters? No, that word is not democracy. Democracy does not appear in the Declaration of Independence, the Constitution or any of the Amendments.

The word is Liberty.

Read your nation's treasures and rediscover for yourself that *Liberty* is an "unalienable Right" and the government is merely the employee whom we have historically hired to "preserve and protect" this Right.

Liberty is not a Supreme Court ruling, a Presidential exemption, a Congressional law or a governmental agency mandate. *Liberty* was "endowed by your creator" and that really does matter. You are American citizens and you have responsibilities and voices. Remind yourself and others often that you and few others on this earth possess: *Liberty*.

Always remember that *Liberty* can be taken away through stealth as well as by force. Those who follow progressive ideals are following paths which are designed to marginalize what was fought for, acquired and now taken for granted.

I believe *Liberty* matters and so should you!.

You and I Will Pay the Piper

Last week, I read the following: "What if we told you those dollar bills in your wallet were not money?" Well, it turns out they are not. They are the national currency of the United States." The bills in our wallets only have value because we believe there is also a corresponding value of gold stored in a safe place for each of the bills we possess. Our currency is really IOU's distributed by our government.

I often purchase a common chocolate wafer snack bar. Recently, this bar doubled in price. Why did a twenty five cent snack suddenly become a fifty cent snack? Please tell me that you didn't immediately scream: "Company Greed". Wrong! It happened because the value of the national currency all Americans hold on faith in our wallets is declining. More unsecured "Federal Reserve Notes" in circulation equals less value. More currency in circulation results in higher prices for everything including the cost of doing business. You have noticed this trend, haven't you?

Our government is daily stealing our currency's value, stealing our future and stealing our faith and trust. We are continuously being sold the insane notion that our nation's multiple trillions of dollars of debt is of no matter because we can simply print more.

How do you develop a strategy against insanity? How do you fight those who act against their own self interest? What weapons can penetrate the ignorance which our *elected progressive leaders* wrap around themselves like a proud mantle?

Understand this: Our faith in our elected progressive leaders will continue to be used against us and it is not them but us who will ultimately pay the piper his due.

History of Uncle Sam

I came across this information about Uncle Sam while searching for something else. I have placed it here because I thought you might find it interesting too. Source: the History Channel for Uncle Sam

On September 7, 1813, the United States received its nickname, Uncle Sam.

The name is linked to Samuel Wilson, a meat packer from Troy, New York, who supplied barrels of beef to the United States Army during the War of 1812. Wilson stamped the barrels with "U.S." for United States, but soldiers began referring to the grub as "Uncle Sam's". The local newspaper picked up on the story and Uncle Sam eventually gained widespread acceptance as the nickname for the U.S. federal government.

In September 1961, the U.S. Congress recognized Samuel Wilson as "the progenitor of America's national symbol of Uncle Sam." Wilson died in 1854 at age 88 and was buried next to his wife Betsy Mann in the Oakwood Cemetery in Troy, New York. The town calls itself "The Home of Uncle Sam".

Perhaps the most famous image of Uncle Sam was created by artist James Montgomery Flagg (1877-1960).

In Flagg's version, Uncle Sam wears a tall top hat and blue jacket and is pointing straight ahead at the viewer.

During World War I, this portrait of Uncle Sam with the words I Want You for the U.S. Army" was used as a recruiting poster. The image, which became immensely popular, was first used on the cover of *Leslie's Weekly* in July 1916 with the title "What Are You Doing for Preparedness?" The poster was widely distributed and has subsequently been re-used numerous times with different captions.

In the late 1860's and 1870's political cartoonist Thomas Nast (1840-1902) began popularizing the image of Uncle Sam. Nast continued to evolve the image, eventually giving Sam the white beard and stars-and-stripes suit that are associated with the character today. The German-born Nast was also credited with creating the modern image of Santa Claus as well as coming up with the donkey as a symbol for the Democratic Party and the elephant as the symbol for the Republican Party. Nast also famously lampooned the corruption of New York City's Tammany Hall in his editorial cartoons and was, in part, responsible for the downfall of Tammany leader William Tweed.

America's Uncle Sam Hospitalized

Following his admission to the hospital today, Uncle Sam quietly admitted he was experiencing painful health issues. He said: "The executive, legislative and judicial branches of my nation's heart are feckless and failing its citizens. They lack initiative, strength of character and are irresponsible."

Continuing slowly and carefully he said the dream carefully described in the Declaration of Independence and The Constitution of the United States is fading. Many citizens have no work, feel alone and have lost hope. My national currency is being devalued at home and in the world. My citizens feel increasingly dependent on government promises based on lies. My nation is accused of practicing racism and economic, social and geographical theft.

Near tears, Uncle Sam then blurted, I lament the impact of the 17th Amendment, the destruction of our health care system, the movement to adopt Common Core's historical inaccuracies and child centered propaganda sold as education reform, unrestrained bureaucratic agencies with countless regulations and the growing acceptance of a dangerous progressive philosophy which is clearly destructive to self reliance while promoting the growth of personal entitlement.

He began coughing violently and his physician quietly added "Uncle Sam is greatly weakened by rampant progressivism. His progressive cancer is like a noxious weed which has deeply hidden roots. However, we can cure him. He will recover and thrive when those roots are pulled from within and destroyed."

My Inner Voice

In 1887, Alexander Tyler, a Scottish history professor at the University of Edinburgh stated: (NOTE: There is much disagreement as to who actually stated the quote below. Who said it is not as important as what was said.)

The average age of the world's greatest civilizations from the beginning of history, has been about 200 years. During those 200 years, these nations have always progressed through the following sequence:

From bondage to spiritual faith
From spiritual faith to great courage
From courage to liberty
From liberty to abundance
From abundance to complacency
From complacency to apathy
From apathy to dependence
From dependence back into bondage

The sand in the clock of our history continues to drain. When the sand empties, the clock will stop. The clock only requires someone to turn it over to begin anew. Civilizations? That is a completely different story. My perception of human life and civilizations tells me that we, you and me, only get one chance to do it right irrespective of our age, color, sexual orientation, monetary worth, political or religious values or beliefs. No matter what happens in the future yet to come, we will all remain in the middle of our own personal caravans. Our past has gone on ahead and the future we will live is trailing swiftly behind. We will always live in the present. What has happened and what will happen are simply parts of now. During our lives we pass the creation back down the lines of the caravan through our presence and our actions.

The United States of America in which I have lived my entire life is fighting for its very existence. The war is being fought both from within and without. I cannot accept and refuse to accept the passing of this great nation. How do I confront it? Do I speak rationally and sadly or do I speak forthrightly and with feeling? My inner voice, the voice of the rational mind, speaks quietly to me and asks me to speak quietly in kind.

The rational, pensive voice I listen to daily speaks using the words and emotions as they are used in Robert Frost's poem, "The Road Not Taken":

> "I shall be telling this with a sigh
> Somewhere ages and ages hence:
> Two roads diverged in a wood, and I
> I took the one less traveled by
> and that has made all the difference."

The other voice I hear, the irrational voice, speaks of personal anger, fear, and mistrust and, yes, even rage. My irrational voice urges me to listen and act with passion. It speaks through the voice and tearful emotion of Marc Antony as he spoke to the masses following Caesar's assassination in William Shakespeare's "Julius Caesar". As Antony spoke in behalf of the fallen leader, he concluded his funeral soliloquy with: "Cry Havoc and let slip the dogs of war!"

What course of action we have taken and what will remain of the United States of America after we are gone is what we wrought by our own hands. For our children and their children, the caravan will have moved on. I hope for them we will have chosen wisely in our past.

A Nuclear Senate Reinstatement Provides A Two Year Window of Security

Two questions were posted and discussed in "Our Caravan" on November 7, 2014.

1. Will the Republican Party take advantage of this opportunity to pronounce the Nuclear Senate established by Harry Reid and the Democratic Party dead in the water or leave it untouched and use it in vengeance against that party?
and
2. When will our president finally come to grips with his personal hubris and truly make an effort to be the leader that this nation needs and deserves?

The Nuclear Senate question is constitutionally, historically and emotionally a complex can of worms. I believe I made an error when I suggested it needed to be dropped. The rational for its removal, however, remains correct. The right to filibuster is important to all of us because it is a protection against the abusive rule and tyranny of those who are a part of a majority. That is why democracies fail and why the United States of America is a republic.

The reinstatement of the Nuclear Senate by the majority Republican Party has a positive side effect. Reinstatement would provide our nation an important two year window of security which can be used to intelligently slow and perhaps turn aside the advancing progressive storm. Reinstatement can always be undone as the soon as the dangers of the next two years of the Obama Presidency have passed us by. With that passing, the door opens to the possibility of a return to the guiding principles, waiting to be found again, in our foundation documents.

We must, therefore, aggressively and successfully confront the fundamental changing of America espoused by our President and his progressive supporters. If we are not successful, the foundation documents will be without value and will be cast aside. Any threats of destruction from outside our nation's borders will immediately become meaningless. The attacking enemy will simply arrive too late. We will have already destroyed ourselves and history will have been proven correct.

The newly elected republican majority in the Senate can and must reinstate the nuclear senate. However, the new Senate majority can and must step forward and pass legislation which effectively opposes and counteracts legislation based on progressive philosophy.

They can and must oppose our current economic insanity.

They can and must re-establish and protect the guaranteed rights and the guiding principles contained in our constitution.

They can and must return us to a nation which values and follows its laws.

They can and must provide clear and effective alternatives and changes to previously enacted legislation and deliver that legislation quickly and directly to the President's desk.

The President could succumb to his hubris and conceivably veto every piece of legislation sent to him by the new majority. In doing so, however, the President risks finishing his term of office wearing his "New Clothes" and holding a shadow legacy.

The second question is by far the easiest to answer because it requires only two words:

Probably never!

The President, Immigration Law, Constitutional Law and the Supreme Court

As this article is being written our nation's president is preparing to go before the nation to announce that he will unilaterally change the currently established immigration law and with the stroke of his pen, he will provide immediate amnesty to millions of people who have broken that immigration law. He has said that he is going to do this because he believes the law needs to be changed and congress has not responded to his personal values and beliefs. He will state, therefore, that he is justified in doing so. His sworn oath of office speaks to the contrary: "*I do solemnly swear (or affirm) that I will faithfully execute the Office of President of the United States, and will to the best of my Ability, preserve, protect and defend the Constitution of the United States.*" We are a nation of laws and I believe the actions of this president are the execution of a planned political power grab and I believe this action is constitutionally wrong and should not be permitted.

This article is intended as a reminder to all of you that the design for this nation provides us with a safety net to be used to examine presidential actions and determine their validity. Our government exists only for the people not for political vanity, posturing or individual power. This is what we are. The teachers I experienced in my youth carefully described in great detail a government of written laws designed to make and keep us free.

The Preamble to our Constitution reads as follows: "**We the People** of the United States, in Order to form a more perfect Union, establish Justice, Insure domestic Tranquility, provide for the common defence (sic), promote the general Welfare, and secure the Blessings of Liberty to ourselves and our Posterity, do ordain and establish this Constitution of the United States of America."

The plan for this nation was not accidental. It was diligently studied, discussed and written. Our constitution established three equal branches of leadership. Each branch has specific written powers and responsibilities and each was designed to prevent the rise of absolute power in any of the other branches. If that horror were to happen, all of the efforts of the framers to secure freedom for them and us would have been in vain. I strongly urge, no, I demand that our nation's Supreme Court, the third and often forgotten branch, to immediately exercise its appointed duty and powers and proceed to closely examine the stated goals and actions of our president in the light of constitutional law. The court's justices must immediately determine for him and all of the members of the Legislative branch and all of the people of this nation that what he has chosen to do is either legal or not legal. The failure of any of the three branches to act as they were intended expands the risk of a great tearing of the fabric of our constitution and the taking of a very large step toward the end of our days as a nation.

How Do You Kill 11 Million People?

During this past week, along with a handshake and a "You will like this book" statement I was handed a copy of How Do You Kill 11 Million People by Andy Andrews. Immediately intrigued and disturbed by the title, I found myself doing a quick overview aimed at trying to discover the true subject matter and reason for such a title. A little over 30 minutes or so later I put the book down convinced that I needed to read it again more carefully. I have since read it not once but twice for good measure. This blog is not so much a review of the book as it is an exploration of the ideas Mr. Andrews carefully researched and cataloged. If you crave a review, I suggest that you turn to Amazon.com and read to your heart's content. The following is as close to a "book review" as I will allow myself to write at this time.

If you are even remotely interested in any of the five discussion points shown below, you should read this book and consider the historical cautions it offers this nation and each of its citizens. Please note and remember that we Americans do not live in a democracy. We live in a constitutional republic.

1. Living in a constitutional republic, we all must understand the power and necessity of truth in government.

2. Living in a constitutional republic, we all must help to reverse the direction that our nation has been taken during the last 100 years.

3. Living in a constitutional republic, we all must demand that our elected leadership in Washington be relentlessly measured in the ballot box against the backdrop of their attack on or support of the constitution.

4. Living in a constitutional republic, we all must learn to overcome our misguided trust in our elected and appointed leaders and reverse the rise in citizen apathy.

5. Living in a constitutional republic, we all must relearn our citizen responsibilities and then practice them.

The State of the Union That You Will Not Hear Tonight

My fellow Americans, I am an ordinary citizen who believes it is necessary to speak of immigration, economics, taxation, character and leadership in a manner that will be lacking from either the heart or mouth of our current President of The United States of America.

Immigration: In spite of those who are choosing to continually rewrite it and denigrate it through falsehoods, the history of this nation is an open truth. The United States has always been a beacon to peoples of this world who long to be free. Our nation's past, with measurable fits and starts, has clearly shown the reality and truth of why immigration and cultural and economic growth go hand in hand. E pluibus unum,"Out of many, one", is not a myth. In fact it was the de facto motto for the United States until 1956 when it was replaced it with "In God We Trust".

You and I are expected to believe and support the untruth that there is no moral and ethical difference between past immigrants and today's. I believe the Immigrants from earlier days were people who really wanted their freedom to be the latch pin of their future as American citizens.

These earlier immigrants wanted to be Americans and they did what they needed to do to have it happen. They did not want to continue to be what they chose to leave.

Today's illegals (That is what they really are.) are people who openly state: I am here and I am going to stay because you cannot or will not stop me and I am entitled to do so. It is in our governments avoidance of written law and the absolute absence of truth that we have created this cultural monster. Look to Europe to see the consequences. We simply cannot continue to exist as a nation by choosing this course. This reality must change or it is all of us who will be forced to change. It will no longer be a united we but a them and an us.

Economics: Question: How do you go broke? Answer: "Slowly and then fast". With very few exceptions, the looming specter of total national economic collapse has much in common with honesty and integrity and the clear understanding that someone will always be better off than you and someone will always be worse off than you. Growing personal and cultural entitlement demands makes zero sense except to those who simply want and a government that provides it in return for a supporting vote.

My wife and I have raised two children who grew up hearing this explanation for the absence of almost everything: We cannot afford it! My wife and I did not add two very important words: **right now**! Hindsight tells me that we should have. I strongly believe most desires, acquisitions and life style changes can all be improved over time through self control and common sense thrift. Many of the desires, acquisitions and life style changes desired by my family looked really good to everyone in our family but they were simply too expensive to risk a possible collapse of the family.

There is no such thing as a free anything and yet individuals, families and your government all want and believe that they are entitled to those wants. Think long and hard right here and now. I believe a national collapse is coming. Would a plan leading to the successful acquisition of something be better than giving into the desire and then facing a collapse? I believe you and the government know the truth.

This country desperately needs people who are capable of saying simply: We cannot afford that right now. We believe that you need that and we will work to make it so but we cannot afford that right now and this is what we are going to do to make it so.

What do you think?

Taxation: I strongly believe that the rationale for taxation is a lie. Taxation was created and originally made the law of the land in 1913 to finance World War 1 and has evolved to support the ideologies of people who redistribute our monies and deem themselves smarter and better than the people like you and me. Do you actually believe that an MIT professor is the only one who thinks you are stupid? Remember this, your taxes do two things that no one in government wants you to hear, know or understand clearly. The money you send to Washington creates jobs for lots and lots of people who *claim* to be hard at work for you. It also creates a larger and larger government and that government stresses and believes that only they can make your life better. Really?

Character and Leadership. Quoting from The Final Summit by Andy Andrews, Abraham Lincoln asks Joan of Arc, "Does adversity build character?" "It does not. If you want to test a person's character, give him power." Continuing, Lincoln says, "Now since we are concerning ourselves here with the very future of humanity, let me add one more thing. Power corrupts. Trust me on this. And because power corrupts, humanity's need for those in power to be of high character increases as the importance of the position of leadership increases. We are discussing character, correct? Not intelligence. Great leadership is a product of great character. And this is why character matters."

Do we reward a man's intentions or his actions?

Demagogues and Economics

I recently read "Defense Against Demagogues" by Walter E. Williams at Townhall.com. I was drawn to this article because it raised two questions in my mind. What is it about demagogues that requires a defense? and How and why can demagogues and economics possibly sit at the same table?

It was demagogues that captured my immediate and complete attention. The word jumped off the page and into my mind and it clearly said: Pay attention here! Mr. Williams strongly illustrated the point that "The greatest tool in the arsenal of demagogues is economic ignorance..." but I came up a little short of understanding the tools in the demagogues arsenal. After a few minutes with a dictionary, a Wikipedia article and a thesaurus, I was also convinced that we do need a defense and I was ready to better understand Mr. Williams' intended message.

This is what I learned during those few minutes and why I decided that a defense against demagogues is required: [from French "demagogue", derived from the Greek "demos" = people/folk and the verb "ago" = carry/manipulate thus "people manipulator"] A demagogue is a political leader who appeals to the emotions, fears, prejudices and ignorance of people in order to gain power and promote political motives.

Demagogues take advantage of a fundamental weakness in a democracy. In a democracy, the ultimate power is held by the people and there is nothing to stop the people from giving power to someone who appeals to the lowest common denominator of a large segment of the population. Relentlessly and without self-restraint, demagogues appeal to the emotions of the poor and the uninformed, pursue personal power, and tell lies to stir up hysteria and exploit crises to intensify popular support for their call to immediate action and increased authority. To enhance their self image, demagogues accuse opponents of weakness and disloyalty to the nation even as they, themselves, are manipulative, bigoted and pernicious.

A defense against demagogues is clearly important to all of us. We need to commit ourselves to learning to recognize and protect ourselves from these people manipulators and we need to increase our understanding and appreciation of economics. We all have a great deal to lose because of our lack of understanding of both.

Advice from Our 1st American to President Obama

Benjamin Franklin is the founder whom I have come to admire and respect the most. Given a choice between a truly historical Benjamin Franklin and our current President, my vote would go to the founder who earned it every day of his life. He was born on January 17, 1706 and died on April 17, 1790. It is reported that 20,000 people attended his funeral. He is often referred to as the 1st American and the "harmonious human multitude".

Compare and contrast Benjamin Franklin with the man whom we elected to this nation's highest position of honor. Our President is but a shadow of the man every American supporter hoped he would be and this nation deserves. Each quotation listed below illustrates specific differences between the man who became this nation's 1st American and the man who became this nation's latest President. It should be easy for you to recognize the differences between the two men. Our President has much to learn about this nation's history, peoples, principles and values. Yet he consistently demonstrates that he cannot or will not do so. Let us hope and pray that the damages he has inflicted on this nation through his goal to change and remake America can yet be repaired. I believe his personal history, his unwillingness to consider that he is wrong and his war against America will prove to be his downfall and will ultimately crush his presidential legacy.

If I were to send a personal letter to President Obama offering him an opportunity to improve his personal legacy and help this nation to grow in his final two years, I would use Franklin quotations to lead him toward a clear understanding of what this nation's peoples deserve from any man but especially the man whom they elected to be their leader of the free world.

The following quotations are from Benjamin Franklin's Wit and Wisdom. Someone will, undoubtedly quibble that this one or that one was not the original work of Franklin. That could be true, but he gave them a flavor of his own.

Note: Each quotation was copied exactly as printed. Quotation marks have been omitted.

None but the well-bred Man knows how to confess a fault, or acknowledge himself in error.

There is much difference between imitating a good man, and counterfeiting him.

Where there is hunger, Law is not regarded; and where Law is not regarded, there will be hunger.

An empty bag cannot stand upright.

Tricks and treachery are the practice of Fools that have not wit enough to be honest.

Observe all men; thyself the most.

Wish not so much to live long, as to live well.

As pride increases, Fortune declines.

Search others for their virtues, thyself for thy Vices.

Clean your Finger, before you point at my spots.

Promises may get thee friends, but non-performance will turn them into enemies.

Duty is not beneficial because it is commanded, but is commanded because it is beneficial.

Those who are feared are hated.

Here comes Glib-Tongue: who can out flatter a dedication; and lie like ten Epitaphs.

A lie stands on one leg, Truth on two.

Wise Men learn by other's harms; Fools by their own.

You may delay, but Time will not.

In Rivers and bad Governments, the lightest things swim at top.

The learned Fool writes his Nonsense in better language than the unlearned but it is still Nonsense.

He is ill clothed that is bare of virtue.

If you would reap Praise you must sow the Seeds, Gentle Words and useful Deeds.

Thou can'st not joke an Enemy into a friend, but thou may'st a Friend into an Enemy.

If you would not be forgotten, as soon as you are dead and rotten, either write things worth reading or do things worth the writing.

Great talkers should be cropped for they have no need of ears.

If you do what you should not you must hear what you would not.

He that scatters thorns let him go barefoot.

Meanness is the Parent of Insolence.

Cunning proceeds from Want of capacity.

You may be too cunning for one, but not for all.

Silence is not always a Sign of Wisdom, but Babbling is ever a Folly.

You may give a Man an Office but you cannot give him Discretion.

The Past Has Always Gone On Before Us

Searching for an explanation and a possible resolution to the problems we are facing as a nation, I have turned to the past that has gone on before us. Do not presume that my journey into events that occurred up to 177 years in our past is wasted effort. Join me here and you will gain a clearer understanding of the intended constitutional role of the President in our history. You will experience a better understanding of what we accomplished, what we believed in the beginning and what we have become. You will be reminded that we are merely the legal inheritors of civil and religious liberty created, fought for and won. You will learn: "We have done nothing to acquire these fundamental blessings which were bequeathed to us by a once hardy, brave and patriotic, but now lamented and departed race of ancestors." We need to change that. Abraham Lincoln, our 16th President, is the most significant person you will meet on our journey: He is there to remind us of the importance of values and principles. He demonstrates personal wisdom and tenacity. And his leadership, when it was most urgently needed, saved our nation from the ignominy of being relegated to the list of our world's nation states that have failed.

I have deliberately used many (emphasis is mine) statements in this document. Rather than viewing them as mere distractions, think of them as specific landmarks that I have posted for your personal consideration. Remember, we are looking for answers to our questions and concerns. Take your time and consider them carefully. In the end, they will make it easier for you to retrace your journey's steps and help you reset your course to a different direction.

While there were others seeking consideration, I have chosen two of Lincoln's historical speeches to be our guides. Web access to these speeches is shown below.

Lincoln's First Inaugural Address: March 4, 1861 and Lincoln's Lyceum Address: January 27, 1838

Lincoln's First Inaugural

"Fellow-Citizens of the United States: In compliance with a custom as old as the Government itself, I appear before you to address you briefly and to take the oath prescribed by the Constitution of the United States to be taken by the President before he enters on the execution of this office." *"I do solemnly swear (or affirm) that I will faithfully execute the Office of President of the United States, and will to the best of my Ability, preserve, protect and defend the Constitution of the United States."* (emphasis is mine)

Even as he carried the weight of a divided nation and the possibility of a great war, Abraham Lincoln observed: *"It is safe to assert that no government proper ever had a provision in its organic law for its own termination. Continue to execute all the express (sic) provisions of our national Constitution, and the Union will endure forever— it being impossible to destroy it, except by some action not provided for in the instrument itself."* (emphasis is mine)

The First Inaugural Address reminded me that the Union is much older than the Constitution. "It was formed, in fact, by the Articles of Association in 1774. It was matured and continued by the Declaration of independence in 1776. It was further matured and the faith of all the then thirteen States expressly plighted and engaged that it should be perpetual, by the Articles of Confederation in 1778. And finally, in 1787, one of the declared objects for ordaining and establishing the Constitution was *"to form a more perfect Union. "* (emphasis is mine)

This is Lincoln's view of presidential responsibility: "The Chief Magistrate derives all of his authority from the people. His duty is to administer the present government as it came into his hands and to transmit it, *unimpaired by him, to his successor.* (emphasis is mine)

The Lyceum Address

Let us now reach further into our past. The date is January 27, 1838. Standing in front of the Young Men's Lyceum of Springfield Illinois audience is 28 year old Abraham Lincoln. His subject for the evening: The Perpetuation of Our Political Institutions.

Lincoln's Lyceum Address focused on citizenship in a democratic republic and possible threats to American institutions. "The speech was brought out by the burning in St. Louis a few short weeks before, by a mob, of a negro. (sic) Lincoln took this incident as a sort of text for his remarks." This speech led the listener toward a better understanding of the destructive effects of mob rule, the effects of a disregard for the rule of law, and the possible creation of a climate ripe for the rise of a potential tyrant. The portion of the speech which most resonated in my mind is the cause and the potential for the rise of this tyrant. I want to make it clear that I am not stating that a perceived, object lesson presented by a 28 year old man is, in fact, being carried out 177 years later. The possibility, however, is interesting and worth pursuing and remembering. *Read the speech in its entirety*.

While you are at it, read the entire Declaration of Independence and read it as often as is necessary for you to understand the vast importance of the very last sentence. *"And for the support of this Declaration, with a firm reliance on the protection of divine Providence, we mutually pledge to each other our lives, our Fortunes and our sacred Honor."* (emphasis is mine)

Like many of you, I have long been familiar with this form of a Lincoln quote: "America will never be destroyed from the outside. If we falter and lose our freedoms, it will be because we destroyed ourselves." An earlier version of this quotation exists in the Lyceum Address and is shown below.

"Shall we expect some transatlantic military giant to step the ocean and crush us at a blow? Never! All the armies of Europe, Asia and Africa combined, with all the treasure of the earth (our own excepted) in their military chest, with a Bonaparte for a commander, could not by force take a drink from the Ohio or make a track on the Blue Ridge in a trial of a thousand years. At what point then is the approach of danger to be expected? I answer. *If it ever reach (sic) us it must spring up amongst us; it cannot come from abroad. If destruction be our lot we must ourselves be its author and finisher. As a nation of freemen we must live through all time or die by suicide."* (emphasis is mine)

"It is to deny what the history of the world tells us is true, to suppose that men of ambition and talents will not continue to spring up amongst (sic) us. And when they do, they will as naturally seek gratification of their ruling passion as others have done before them.

The question then is, Can that gratification be found in supporting and maintaining an edifice that has been erected by others? Most certainly it cannot. Many great and good men, sufficiently qualified for any task they should undertake, may ever be found whose ambition would aspire to nothing beyond a seat in Congress, a gubernatorial or a presidential chair; but such belong not to the family of the lion or the tribe of the eagle. What! Think you these places would satisfy an Alexander, a Caesar, or a Napoleon? Towering genius disdains a beaten path. It seeks regions hitherto unexplored. It sees no distinction in adding story to story upon the monuments of fame erected to the memory of others. It denies that it is glory enough to serve under any chief. It scorns to tread in the footsteps of any predecessor, however illustrious. It thirsts and burns for distinction; and if possible, it will have it, whether at the expense of emancipating slaves or enslaving freemen. Is it unreasonable, then, to expect that some man possessed of the loftiest genius, coupled with ambition sufficient to push it to its utmost stretch, will at some time spring up among us? And when such a one does, *it will require the people to be united with each other, attached to the government and laws and generally intelligent to successfully frustrate his designs."* (emphasis is mine)

"Distinction will be his paramount object, and although he would as willingly, perhaps more so, acquire it by doing

good as harm, yet, that opportunity being past, and nothing left to be done in the way of building up, he would set boldly to the task of pulling down." (emphasis is mine)

In its entirety, the Lyceum Address looks to the future of the United States by stating "the past must fade, is fading, has faded with the circumstances that produced it." Lincoln takes special note of the founding leaders and their history and he proclaims them gone. But wait! Here is the rest of the story. Here is the key to saving and recreating the United States which many, like me, are trying to find.

"They (the founders) were the pillars of the temple of liberty; and now that they have crumbled away, that temple must fall UNLESS we, their descendants, supply their places with other pillars, hewn (sic) from the solid quarry of sober reason. Passion has helped us, but it can do no more. In the future it will be our enemy. *Reason, cold, calculating, unimpassioned reason, must furnish all the materials for our future defence.* (sic) Let those materials be moulded (sic) into: *General Intelligence, Sound Morality, and in particular, A reverence for the constitution and laws; and, That we improved to the last; That we remained free to the last ; that we revered; his name to the last; that, during his long sleep, we permitted no hostile foot to pass over or desecrate his resting place;*

shall be that which to learn the last trump shall awaken our Washington." (emphasis is mine)

Lincoln ended his address with these words:

"Upon these let the proud fabric of freedom rest, as the rock of its basis; as truly as has been said of the only other greater institution, "the gates of hell shall not prevail against it" (emphasis is mine)

The emphasized words sound kind of familiar don't they?

Can't place them? Google them or try Matthew 16 -18.

"Our Caravan" has helped me to remember that at any moment I am standing in the present and the future is but an instant behind. The people, lessons and events of the past are all still moving on ahead of me. I stand in awe of those people and what they learned, understood and endured. I have no idea where we will arrive as we join them and become the past but I do know that our arrival will be determined by the important choices we have made along the way.

What you and I will leave behind as a gift remains to be created. Hopefully it will be needed and eventually discovered by those others who have not yet taken their place in Our Caravan.

Supreme Court Justices Should Have Term Limits

The title of the article caught my eye and I read it and felt its truth. "Give judges terms, not lifetime appointments" appeared in the Wednesday, August 5, 2015 edition of The Detroit News. It was written by Doug Bandow, a graduate of Stanford Law School and a senior fellow at the Cato Institute. The Cato Institute is a Public Policy Think Tank dedicated to the principles of individual liberty. Bandow wrote "It is time to impose accountability while preserving independence." "Judges are supposed to play a limited though vital role – interpreting, not transforming the law". "Limiting the term of office for Supreme Court justices from a life time event to a finite fixed terms number of years, would simultaneously achieve both objectives."

I support Bandow's position that we need to reign in the Supreme Court's increasingly common practice of making public policy instead of judging the constitutionality of the issues brought before it. Our nation is a nation of laws and there is a specific written plan in place to create, manage and verify those laws. The name of the plan is The Constitution of the United States. It is clear to me that the Congressional branch exists to create necessary laws. The Executive branch exists to execute the laws created by

Congress. The Supreme Court exists to judge the constitutionality of laws. I also support the Cato Institute's efforts because I believe it is our possession of individual liberties that keeps our nation from jumping off the track.

Why do the nine member justices forming the Supreme Court find it so difficult to state that a specific issue submitted to the court for examination is either supported by the Constitution or it is not? Surely, "partisan leanings" is not the issue. If the issue brought before the court is judged to be supported by the Constitution then it is lawful. If it is not supported by the Constitution, it is unconstitutional. The court should simply determine exactly why or how it failed to meet the constitutionality test and send it back to congress or to its original source to be revised in a manner determined to be acceptable under the framework of the Constitution. I have yet to discover anything written in the Constitution that gives the justices the prerogative to change the meaning or the intent of the words used to create the law or issue submitted by others who are not of the court.

Article 3, section 1 of the Constitution of the United States defines the judicial power of the United States. There are several capitalized words in the copied Constitutional language below which might appear to you to be incorrectly capitalized but they are shown here as they appear in the Constitution. Please note this is the section which Doug Bandow's article addresses. There are, in fact, two more sections in Article 3 of the Constitution. Section 2 lists the extent of judicial authority extended to the court and section 3 defines Treason. Finally, note in line two of section 1 shown below that only "Congress may ordain and establish" other courts.

"The judicial Power of the United States shall be vested in one supreme Court, and in such inferior Courts as the Congress may from time to time ordain and establish. The judges, both of the supreme and inferior Courts, shall hold their office during good behavior, and shall at stated Times, receive for their Services a Compensation, which shall not be diminished during the Continuance in Office."

Did you know? The two word "Good behavior" phrase has been historically interpreted to mean that judges may serve for the remainder of their lives. Justice William Orville Douglas from Yakima, Washington holds the record for continuous service. He served an astounding 36 years and 209 days from April 17, 1939 to November 12, 1975.

Did you know? Supreme Court justices may be impeached if they do not maintain "Good behavior". In our republic, all impeachments are initiated in the House of Representatives and all are tried in the Senate. In our entire history, Samuel Chase holds the distinction of being the only Supreme Court justice to have been impeached. He was impeached by the United States House of

Representatives on March 12, 1804 for allegedly letting his "partisan leanings" affect his Court decisions. Chase was acquitted by the Senate on March 1, 1805.

Slavery, War, Immigration and the Rule of Law

The 14th Amendment to our nation's constitution was passed by Congress June 13, 1866 and Ratified July 9, 1868. In his book <u>American Founding Son: John Bingham and the Invention of the Fourteenth Amendment</u>, Gerard N. Magliocca, a professor of law at Indiana University, identifies the Ohio politician John Bingham as the man who drafted the crucial language of that 14th Amendment. He specifically identified Bingham as the man who is responsible for the words: "No state shall make or enforce any law which shall abridge the privileges or immunities of citizens of the United States; nor shall any state deprive any person of life, liberty, or property, without due process of law; nor deny to any person within its jurisdiction the equal protection of the laws."

Two national, historical issues needed to be resolved prior to the creation of the 14th Amendment in 1866. As Abraham Lincoln stated, "A house divided against its self cannot stand". The Civil War, 1861 - 1865, was fought to keep this nation whole and existing slavery could not be allowed to expand. Slavery of any person is an evil wrong. Our Declaration of Independence declares for all time that "all men are created equal, that they are endowed by their Creator with certain unalienable Rights" and yet, slavery existed. Our written history shows us that slavery existed before the Constitution was written and it was allowed, by agreement, to continue so that this nation could be born. However, slavery is not even mentioned in our Constitution. It was believed in time slavery would fade away. It did not fade in the southern states. It flourished and it could not be allowed to expand to this nation's western growth.

The endured human suffering required to correct these wrongs was monumental and traumatic. David Hacker a demographic historian from Binghamton University in New York states that "at least 750,000 lives were lost during the Civil War." Among those who died were the widely unwelcome Irish and German immigrants who had only recently arrived here legally in pursuit of their desire to become citizens. If you believe that this generation's immigration concerns are unique, examine the infusion of the Irish and the Germans to these shores. It is a powerful immigration story in itself. Look it up.

History shows us that the Civil War was not enough to remove slavery and Lincoln's Emancipation Proclamation delivered on January 1, 1863 was not enough. The door to slavery remained open in the south and it needed to be closed. When ex-Confederate States originally refused to ratify the 14th Amendment, John Bingham crafted a legislative compromise that ordered the Union Army to organize new elections across the South that would include African-Americans. He told the House that "unless you put [the South] in terror of your laws, made efficient by the solemn act of the whole people to punish the violators of oaths, they will defy your restricted legislative power when reconstructed." Bingham's legacy is best summarized by a speech that he gave as a young man. In it, he said: "When the vital principle of our government, the equality of the human race, shall be fully realized, when every fetter within our borders shall be broken and a noble mission fulfilled, we may call to the down-trodden and oppressed of all lands — come."

I am fairly certain that if he were alive today, Bingham would choose the support of law even as he would welcome the downtrodden with open arms. Take the time to read the entire 14th Amendment and show me where he perceived national justice for all to mean to break existing law. The former slaves and their children were finally, in fact and law, United States citizens. The state in which they lived no longer mattered. Former slaves were to be afforded the same rights and protections as any other citizen in all states. In its time, the 14th Amendment had dramatically closed the door to the past and moved us another step forward toward a final closure. Slavery, the unsolved issue that divided this nation from its very beginning had been legally resolved. However, the 14th Amendment, while appropriate for 1866, could not and did not anticipate other divisive issues of race and immigration which have appeared at various times in our history and a new one exists today. The entry of non legal peoples of a non European descent and their progeny is causing us much angst today and Bingham and other national leaders of 1866 had absolutely no way to anticipate this reality. Consider this: *Slavery is a historical forced immigration inflicted on many races by this world's nation states.* It was ultimately banished from this country through the powerful force of human will and law.

The United States is a self defined nation of laws. Our Laws are one of the core principles of our very existence. Individuals and families who have chosen to follow the course of legal immigration have, in fact and law, demonstrated their support of this core principle. They are valuable and should be welcomed with open arms. It is, indeed our noble mission to call to the down trodden and oppressed of all lands. However, this nation must find a way to stand up and reaffirm its laws or lose its way. The path to freedom will be closed forever to those of the world who would join us in our pursuit and to us as well. The alternative is not acceptable. Illegal is not legal by definition. Allowing those who have come to this country illegally is by definition unlawful. Even so, illegal peoples continue to arrive and they continue to claim guaranteed rights created for United States citizens. The claiming of individual and family rights by illegal peoples should not be permitted, supported or encouraged. These practices are destructive and divisively dangerous to legal citizens and they are a detriment to our national core principles.

I have grown weary waiting for the Supreme Court to speak in support or rejection of existing Immigration law. In my mind, it is absolutely predictable that the court's nine appointed justices will simply continue to speak and vote as they always have. They will continue to vote with strict adherence to their philosophical and political support base. They will continue to sing to the choir that selected them to be members of this very special legal fraternity. Not one justice appears to be willing to forgo the guaranteed lifelong position that is theirs by appointment if they "remain in good Behavior" and do not upset the applecart. A court appointment should now be perceived as the second highest level political plum tree in this nation and the longest lasting.

I am also weary of the court's refusal to confront our "I'll do it alone with my phone and pen" president who has wowed the masses with his politically magical left hand even as his right hand continues to provide gifts for votes. Remember this: The Executive Branch carefully detailed in our Constitution exists to execute this nation's laws, not to create them. Only Congress can create laws. In the absence of the rule of law Obama will have nothing left to skirt and he will ultimately achieve his primary goal to remake America. Remember it was this president who proclaimed "We are five days away from fundamentally transforming the United States of America." I remain convinced that the allowed presidential directive in support of illegal immigration is a malformed tree that will put down roots. The fruits of this tree will prove to be very bitter. I also see all illegal presence as a negative weight on the left side of the scale of justice and I perceive the hand of progressivism lingering patiently in the scale's shadow.

Too many of us only perceive the practice of law as secret and mysterious and understood by few. I see the common image of law balanced by justice and think: If only the blindfolded lady, "Lady Justice", could see and finally speak through the mighty "Sword of Justice" she carries in her right hand.

Three Questions for Your Consideration

Question 1: Which of the following scenarios describes the most profound personal loss?

Scenario 1: You know that you possess something important and fragile and it is being slowly taken away from you but you do not know what it is. In a moment of clarity, you discover what you are losing and understand it is almost too late to stop the taker.

Scenario 2: You have lived your entire adult life believing and pursuing something so marvelous and rare that others in this world choose to risk death each and every day to possess it and you feel it slipping through your fingers.

Second Question: What is being stolen?
Third Question: Who or what is the thief?

I believe most of you take this word for granted but you do know it when you see it or think about it. I believe that some of you will probably know it but will not understand it until it is gone. Its loss to you and all who follow after you is something worthy of your consideration.

All I ask you to do is to rediscover the word and consider its value to all of us. Grab a mirror! The word is *ytrebil*.

Freedom: Past Present and Future

Several well known people are on record predicting the 2016 election cycle will become historically recognized and remembered as the most important election in our nation's history. They also predict the possibility of a historical turning point, a possible point of crisis and, perhaps, a point of no return.

If these predictions are accurate, it is you "the people" who must choose to affirm that you cherish what you currently possess. Your failure to vote in the company of wisdom will significantly open wide the door that protects you from those who desire to make our Constitution worth nothing more than the quaint ideas of people long dead. Your nation and your world envied way of life hangs in the balance. Are you up to it? Let's get started. The following is a short list of questions important to your survival as a free person.

Your future and mine are found in the quests below.

Can you name each branch of the government and define its constitutional responsibilities?

Can you completely define the phrase "unalienable rights" from the Declaration of Independence? Hint: It means much more than they cannot be taken away.

Which historical document contains the phrase "Separation of Church and State"? (Constitution, Declaration of Independence or Neither)

Which government branch is constitutionally designated to approve Cabinet and Supreme Court appointments? How many votes are required for approval? Why?

Look to the Bill of Rights and answer the next four questions. They reveal the very heart of what progressives and self identified socialists strongly desire to take away from you.

Can you explain the 1st Amendment as written?

Can you explain the 2nd Amendment as written?

Can you explain the 4th Amendment as written?

Can you explain the 10th Amendment as written?

A Progressive is too Big to Swallow

"Poor old lady, she swallowed a fly.
I don't know why she swallowed a fly.
Poor old lady, I think she'll die."

In an ever increasing frenzy the Poor old lady continues to swallow a menagerie of ever larger insects and animals. Each stanza ends with the same observation. "I think she'll die". In the seventh and final stanza, the frenzy ends.

"Poor old lady, she swallowed a horse.
She died, of course."

> The "Poor old Lady" by Anonymous: The Poetry Foundation

Unless "We the people" turn aside from the incremental step by step progressive rights consuming frenzy, "She died, of course" will predictably and appropriately be written on the tombstone of our nation laid to waste because it foolishly self destroyed its historical beginnings, its strength and, in due course, itself.

The Declaration of Independence of July 4, 1776 gave all of us the solid foundation of "equality under the law" and it has nurtured us ever since. *"We hold these truths to be self-evident, that all men are created equal, that they are endowed by their Creator with certain unalienable Rights, that among these are Life, Liberty and the pursuit of Happiness."*

It is our right is to pursue happiness. Happiness, however, is not guaranteed!

The foundation's lesson is clear. Progressives, however, actually disdain the declaration's premise that all people are equal as people and we, therefore, have the right to "equality under the law" as its accepted meaning. Remember, this specific equality did not exist in all of history before this declaration was written. Progressives now challenge the "equality under law" interpretation. They are trying to substitute this impartial definition with the artificial equalities of "results" and "conditions" and postulate that the envied resources and perceived advantages earned and possessed by others actually belong to all by "right of existence"!

Progressivism, Socialism and a Dark Future

It is nearly impossible for me to not laugh outrageously and then convulse in tears of sadness as I view the incredible gullibility of the supporters of current democratic party candidates and by extension Obama and all progressives existing in both political parties past and present. For all peoples who choose to follow progressivism and or socialism, their personal freedoms, choice and self determination are soon to be replaced by servitude to the state. Differences of definition, language and anticipated outcomes of progressivism and socialism, as they are currently being presented as rightful replacements for our nation's constitution, are very slight. And yet, Socialism is clearly the next anointed and preplanned step in the process to captivate and enslave the masses who simply do not understand or appreciate what they already possess.

The poem shown below popped into my mind and it speaks volumes of practical truth and the truth has never been a consideration of the foes of freedom.

Cruel Clever Cat

Sally, having swallowed cheese,
Directs down holes the scented breeze,
Enticing thus, with baited breath
Nice mice to an untimely death.

Geoffrey Taylor

With deep sadness, I have come to believe our nation's colleges and universities are in fact the primary source of applied political correctness and progressive thinking.

These institutions have also opened the door to legitimize socialism. Socialism is, by definition, *"a political and economic theory of social organization that advocates that the means of production, distribution and exchange should be owned or regulated by the community as a whole."*

"Socialism should be considered a transitional social state between the overthrow of capitalism and the realization of communism." Make no mistake here! "Community" is, in reality, the State and the State is our elected government and any government, unchecked, is power without freedom!

It is frightening to watch young people turn away from capitalism and their nation's history and speak in support of dual philosophies which are both alien and destructive toward the guaranteed personal freedoms that have been theirs since birth. They seem to be doing the unthinkable with zero comprehension of what is being laid before them as their entitlement.

I urge all Americans to pursue the light of freedom and relish in its warmth. Do so with the realization that you possess the tools necessary to escape a predictably dark future.

Woodrow Wilson's Progressive Legacy In Question

Just in case you missed it! Look for the article "Utah Senate Votes to Repeal 17th Amendment" by Christine Rousselle at Townhall.com for February 26. The Utah Senate voted 20-6 to ask the Congress to repeal the 17th Amendment. Why is this significant? "The 17th Amendment was not what the founders of the country had intended and changed the meaning of the role of the senators." This vote is but a small step in a long necessary journey, but it is significant because the very foundation of our Republic was forever weakened by the creation of the 17th Amendment.

This news is good reason to believe that the significance of the language of the Constitution as originally conceived, written and adopted is finally being reexamined and understood. It is not a living document subject to change because of time and circumstance. Perhaps, if only perhaps, the conceived Republic as written and defined might yet receive a life saving transfusion of truth and understanding.

To better understand this Utah vote, turn your thinking to 1913. It was a wonderful year for Woodrow Wilson and all progressives and a horrible setback for those who side with Freedom.

In 1913, Progressives laid the necessary foundations for the intended growth of their basic mind numbing philosophy. The progressive legislative agenda was built with the support of three major pieces of legislation. All three came to fruition in 1913. Two pieces changed our Constitution and the third provided the perceived bottomless pit of money necessary to accomplish their goals.

Piece number 1: 16th Amendment FEDERAL INCOME TAX

This allowed the federal government a steady flow of money and removed any further action required by the states.

Piece number 2: 17th Amendment A DIRECT VOTE OF THE PEOPLE FOR STATE SENATORS INSTEAD OF STATE APPOINTMENTS.

This amendment removed the ability of the states as political bodies to limit federal power.

Piece number 3: THE FEDERAL RESERVE WAS CREATED. The FED can print money on demand. This allowed theoretically unlimited leverage on paper money without the acquiescence of Congress.

Enter Stage Left

"All the world's a stage,
And all men and women merely players;
They have their exits and their entrances,
And one man in his time plays many parts…"
                    "As You Like It" Act II Scene VII
                    William Shakespeare, 1564 -1616

Our nation's men and women are troubled and struggling with what they are seeing, hearing or experiencing first hand. It is not difficult to understand why. Neither is it difficult to notice that many have turned, in desperation, to the safety of "I wish" for solace. There are several problems with I wish. The most obvious is the old adage "Be careful what you wish for because you just might get it."

History is filled with men and women who pinned their desperation, hopes and wishes on the likely existence of an all powerful elixir. Elixir has been defined as a flavored liquid used for medicinal purposes. Ancient alchemists also sought a preparation that was believed capable of changing metals into gold. Others sought a preparation to induce love. The early Greeks saw it as a powder for drying wounds. Elixir was sought by many because it was believed that the right combinations of unlike extracts, tinctures and powders would, when matched correctly, cure all diseases. The wish and therefore the hope for the "cure all" was widely sold to many who had become convinced enough to believe and trust. Most of the believers merely discovered they had been cheated. Many of them died.

The word flimflam comes to us from old Norse as a lampoon or mockery. During the sixteenth century it was understood to be nonsense or idle talk and a sort of shallow trick that a reasonable person wouldn't fall for. To the unwary, the flimflam man created distractions to confuse his target customer even as he was being shortchanged. Flimflam is often found in the company of claptrap. Claptrap is defined as cheap, showy language, pure nonsense and silly rubbish. It is almost always displayed by hucksters several of which we identify as political candidates. In all of the current debates, both republican and democratic, aired on television to date, I have seen few leaders emerge from behind the shadow of flimflam and claptrap. The daily interactive verbal battle ground leading to the most important office in the free world litters the landscape with wishful thinking, magic, flimflam, claptrap and more than a dash of hyperbole and dishonesty.

We are, therefore, on a collision course with history and in spite of current revisionists, history never gets it wrong.

Observe the current outcomes created by political hucksters preying on the trusting people who chose to believe in them:

The reality of spending our future with money printed on demand,

The true cost of something for nothing schemes,

The pain suffered through the loss of self worth and self respect,

The tyranny of a top down government,

The massive underemployment in response to regulations promulgated by agencies accountable to no one,

Historically continuously improving peaceful race relations of this nation have been reduced to confrontations with the promise of open hostility a simple breath away,

Our internationally respected health program is being dismantled piece by piece,

We face the misuse of constitutionally entrusted power, and

We have ignored our national moral and ethical compasses and the constitutional door built for our safety and our eventual national maturity is rapidly closing and history is patiently waiting to push the reset button.

We could accidentally and suddenly rediscover what made us great for such a long time but that too is probably nothing more than wishful thinking. It could be a very long dark night. Perhaps forever!

Truth as a Journey on a Winding Road

I usually turn to a search of current and historical truths when I am confronted by written and spoken words in direct opposition to what I was taught and believe to be true. I am one of those people who simply need to verify what we believe. In doing so I often learn more than what I thought I knew before I started. Truth is easily accessed by using the six single word questions used by good journalists: Who, What, When, Where, How, and the all important Why. After the search, the newly learned or perhaps merely forgotten results often cause me to pause and reflect and think to myself, I guess I really didn't know that.

I began with David Barton's book The Jefferson Lies: Exposing the Myths You've Always Believed About Thomas Jefferson. Barton's book confronts revisionist's writings dedicated to attacks on our nation's founders, especially Thomas Jefferson, as evil slave owners. I found obvious truth to the contrary to the words of revisionists and a new reading of Thomas Paine's timeless masterpiece, Common Sense, reminded me of the clearly stated reasons for our separation from England. A quick review of the history behind the Bill of Rights surprised me yet again. The questions asked and answered, once again, proved refreshing.

My journey continued with Scott Rohter's January 2012 article "Life, Liberty and the Divisive Issue of Slavery". Rohter captured my attention when he immediately asked "Why did the Founding Fathers use the words Life, Liberty and the Pursuit of Happiness in the Declaration of Independence instead of the words Life, Liberty and Property? Slaves were certainly considered as property.

Why indeed. Life Liberty and Property are found in English common law and the writings of English philosopher, John Locke. Locke's written ideas became the foundation of the Whig Party in America and these words are also the original language source for the Declaration of Independence. Clearly, Thomas Jefferson, John Adams and Benjamin Franklin, the primary drafters of the Declaration of Independence, avoided taking a position either in favor or against slavery by substituting "the Pursuit of Happiness" for Property for good reason.

Also for clear and good reason, slave state property rights were not mentioned as one of the "self-evident truths" and a part of the "unalienable rights" endowed by our Creator.

When carefully read, Article 1, Section 2, and Clause 3 of the Constitution get at the heart of the matter.

It was clear that the six Southern states would never have agreed to ratify the Constitution because the language threatened their property rights. The remaining seven northern states did not wish to "prolong the unconscionable sin of slavery" nor support property rights which included the ownership of people. In fact, most northerners felt that the whole idea of *owning* another person was wrong."

In the attempt to build a nation, it was recognized that the issue of slavery was not to be decided at that time. It was recognized for what it was but change could come later. There was a nation waiting to be born. It was not an act of hypocrisy or malice. The founders merely postponed the confrontation of the issue. There is no reason to believe that these men supported the concept or reality of slavery. It can and has been demonstrated that there was a strongly held belief that the Southern states would come to understand the error of their ways and a nation could be given life. Sadly, while this evenly considered approach to the issue of slavery eventually led to the ratification of the Constitution, it also proved powerless to change the minds of those who continued to hold their human property.

Our Constitution was written in the summer of 1787. Rhode Island did not even send delegates to this convention. Even that was not a done deal. By 1788 only 9 states had ratified the Constitution. On June 21, 1788 New Hampshire was the ninth state to ratify our Constitution. *Article VII of the Constitution states: "The Ratification of the Conventions of nine States (sic), shall be sufficient for the Establishment of this Constitution between the States so ratifying the Same."* The government began on March 4, 1789.

James Madison promised that the bill of rights would be added after ratification. In June 1789, Madison finally kept his promise and proposed a series of amendments to be debated in the first Congress and we had our first ten amendments to the Constitution. Virginia, New York, North Carolina and Rhode Island were the last four states to ratify.

You need to be reminded that the commitment to ratify by the nine was absolutely necessary. Without the agreement and support of the nine we would have had no Constitution. The founders did what was expedient to bring states and peoples together to build a nation not to perpetuate a wrong. They were not racists.

We are all aware that another crisis would arise in the form of a Civil War beginning in 1861. This dramatic conflict again focused on owned property and it came at a great cost but it did finally move the will of the nation forward again and away from slavery.

The search for truth is almost always a journey on a winding road and I eventually found myself focusing on The Bill of Rights because its creation insured that all thirteen colonies not just the original nine as noted above would eventually ratify the Constitution and set our nation on its desired course. Clearly it was not a short journey.

There are but two brief points remaining for your consideration:

First, History clearly reveals that "Democrats believed in owning slaves. Republicans did not." How, then, can we explain the polar shift now voiced today. Democrats are today's self proclaimed race protectors.

Second: From the *Billofrightsinstitute.org/founding documents/constitutional*, James Madison is quoted as seeing at least one important difference between European freedom documents and our Constitution. "In Europe, charters of liberty have been granted by power. America has set the example of charters of power granted by liberty."

The Electoral College

Andrew Jackson (1824), Samuel J. Tilden (1876), Grover Cleveland (1888) and Al Gore (2000) all won the national popular vote in the election years following their names but each failed to become President of the United States. The cause for each loss has been examined and linked to a constitutional process known as The Electoral College.

Three strongly held presidential beliefs from our early beginnings are perfectly clear. First, it was believed that the selection of a president should be the responsibility of those who were most knowledgeable and informed from each state. Randall G. Holcomb put it this way: "The process was never intended to be democratic. The first presidents were appointed by elites, not elected by the masses…" Secondly, the selection was to be determined "solely on merit and without regard to State of origin or political party." Third, "The office should seek the man the man should not seek the office".

Consider the historical context of a nation just getting started. We were a nation of 13 new states wanting to be in charge of their own destiny and each possessing a low trust of a "national government". We had a much smaller population and it was spread out across a thousand miles from north to south. We experienced very real poor modes of transportation and we experienced poor communications with each other. On the other hand, we created this nation without the presence of established political parties because political parties were extended very little respect.

The beginnings of the Electoral College can be traced to the 1787 Constitutional Convention. That convention, sometimes called the Philadelphia Convention, took place between May 25 and September 17, 1787 and remains as the only one ever called in United States history. During this convention, the delegates found a common ground compromise between three possible methods of selecting a president. Only experts would be designated to select the president and the vice president.

Methods of selecting considered by the Convention:

1. *Congress should choose the president.* This was rejected because of potential "hard feelings", "political bargaining", possible "corruption", possible "interference from foreign powers" and "balance of power between legislative and executive branches".

2. *State legislatures should choose the president.* This was rejected because the president might find cause to "beholden to the State legislatures" and the possible dilution of "federal authority."

3. *A direct popular vote should choose the president*. This was rejected because it was feared "that without sufficient information about candidates from outside their State, people would naturally vote for a 'favorite son' from their state or region."

The language used in Article II, Section 1 of the Constitution shown below created the foundation for the implementation of the Electoral College "experts" concept.

Article II Section 1

"Each state shall appoint, in such a Manner as the legislature thereof may direct, a Number of Electors, equal to the whole number of Senators and Representatives to which the State may be entitled in Congress; but no Senator or Representative, or Person holding an Office of Trust or Profit under the United States, shall be appointed as an Elector."

The term *"Electoral College" does not appear in the Constitution nor does it appear in Amendment XII* which became clearly necessary following the results of the election of 1800. At that time each candidate for president and vice president ran alone. The presidential electors of 1800 (the Electoral College) failed to "distinguish between the office of president and vice president on their ballots" Thomas Jefferson won the presidential election with 73 electoral votes. Aaron Burr running as the vice president candidate with Thomas Jefferson also received 73 votes for president making the vote for the presidency a tie. In the case of a tie the Constitution requires an election to be decided in the House of Representatives. Jefferson finally won but only after 36 votes. Amendment XII to the Constitution was written and ratified to ensure that the electors make a discrete choice between their selections for president and vice president.

While confusing to many people, when Americans vote for a President and Vice President, they are actually voting for presidential electors, known collectively as the Electoral College. It is these electors, chosen by the people, who elect the chief executive. The Constitution assigns each state a number of electors equal to the combined total of the state's Senate and House of Representatives delegations. The Electoral College consists of 538 electors. 170 electoral votes, an absolute majority of one more than half of the total electors, is required to elect the President and Vice President. The process for selecting electors varies throughout the United States. Generally, the political parties nominate electors at their State party conventions or by a vote of the party's central committee in each State. Electors are often selected to recognize their service and dedication to their political party. They may be State-elected officials, party leaders, or persons who have a personal or political affiliation with the Presidential candidate.

This is what happens to the vote you cast in the popular election of a President:

"After the November election your governor prepares a 'Certificate of Ascertainment' listing all of the candidates who ran for President in your state along with the names of the respective electors. The certificate declares the winning candidate in your state and shows which electors will represent your state at the meeting of the electors. Your state's certificates of Votes are sent to the Congress of the National Archives as part of the official records of the presidential election. Each state's electoral votes are counted in a joint session of Congress on the 6th of January in the year following the meeting of the electors. Members of the House and Senate meet in the House Chamber to conduct the official tally of electoral votes. The Vice President, as President of the Senate, presides over the count and announces the results of the vote. The President of the Senate then declares which persons, if any, have been elected President and Vice President of the United States."

Article II Section I of the Constitution was seen as in the best interest of the United States by the founders. It cannot simply be removed because it is a part of the original Constitution. There have been several other election processes offered but none have been passed by Congress and sent to the States for ratification as a Constitutional amendment.

A Convention to propose amendments to the United States Constitution is also called an Article V Convention, or Amendments Convention. Under the most common method for amending the Constitution, an amendment must be proposed by a two-thirds majority in both houses of Congress and ratified by three-fourths of the states.

Carefully read Article V of the Constitution shown below. There is a second method. The second method is less familiar to most people, because it has never been used. The language makes it perfectly clear that the several states legislatures have been given the same rights as Congress to call for a convention to consider amendments to the Constitution.

Article V language follows below:

"The Congress, whenever two thirds of both Houses shall deem it necessary, shall propose Amendments to this constitution, *or, on the Application of the Legislatures of the several States,* shall call a Convention for proposing Amendments, which in either Case shall be valid to all Intents and Purposes, as part of this Constitution, when ratified by the Legislatures of three fourths of the several States, or by Conventions in three fourths thereof, as one or the other Mode of Ratification may be proposed by Congress..."

Hopefully this article has led you to a better understanding of your Constitution and the Electoral College process.

I do not believe the Constitution of the United States is out dated or quaint, or a living document subject to change with the times. I remain in awe of the skillful men who nurtured it from draft through its eventual ratification on June 21, 1788. Those men gave us a gift which keeps on giving. It remains in my mind as a national map. From its ratification to today our Constitution is 228 years old and is still here *to protect us from ourselves*.

Progressives versus Truth in Trump Campaign

Television's X Files stated "The truth is out there". Truth is earthbound too but as Ayn Rand has pointed out, "The truth is not for all men but only for those who seek it."

Donald Trump, not my favorite primary candidate, benefitted greatly from progressive media's feigned supportive coverage. He won his party's presidential primary, possibly because his opponents became almost invisible in the hours of progressive media's free exposure. However, Mr. Trump apparently failed to comprehend visual and print media's profit and manipulation motives for providing it. Profiting from their clearly Cheshire cat coverage of his campaign these media outlets will now reuse what he did and said to win the Republican nomination to destroy him and again turn a profit and manipulate desired outcomes. Consciously observe progressive media joined at the hip by progressives from both political parties. They are conspiring to hand "The Donald" his own head on a platter and Time magazine presented him as a wax caricature's melting head. This is the American version of the highly stylized Japanese dance drama called Kabuki.

Lost in all of this high drama is the yet to be determined historical cost to all of those once passive, quiet people who perceived in him a man committed to representing what they felt was theirs by virtue of "unalienable" and "endowed by their creator" rights spelled out in our founding documents and our nation's history Those people took a collective inward breath and turned wildly demonstrative and he rode their wave. With his and the people's voices now being marginalized and ridiculed, the word of the day in all of progressive media is *Gotcha!*

Progressive media's manipulations are neither the beginning nor the end of this story. Unfortunately, the worst is yet to come.

OOPs! An update is now required. (November 9, 2016) The citizens living on the lands between the mountains and separated from major cities have turned this country on its ear. They heard and they believed that with their vote, things could be changed for the better. There is now a warming glow of a rising sun and not the shadow of a setting sun and there is the presence of the rising tide necessary for the ship of state to float and seek new harbors. For a while I will wear a smile and watch closely. It remains a long time to Friday, January 20, 2017.

Free Speech Is an Unalienable Right

One man's refusal to stand for the Star Spangled Banner before an NFL football game began as a personal protest. That is his guaranteed right. Fueled by personal conscience and anger his visible silent protest has, as of this writing, now spread to every corner of our nation.

At the very core of this protest is Amendment 1 of this nation's Bill of Rights born of necessity because the founders sought a way to prevent misconstruction or abuse of its powers and to secure *the beneficent ends of the institution* which is our government.

Amendment 1 *"Congress shall make no law respecting an establishment of religion, or prohibiting the free exercise thereof, or abridging the freedom of speech or the press, or of the people peacefully to assemble, and to petition the Government for redress of grievances."* (Ratified On December 15, 1791)

Lost in almost every published discussion related to this protest is the obvious lack of understanding of the intent of the 1st Amendment. The amended Constitution does not say that you have to like, approve or support what someone does or says.

It does, however, clearly guarantee *the words or demonstrations of individuals or groups as a method of protest are supported and protected by the Constitution*. Your choice to support or attack this guaranteed right is important to all of us and has potential consequences.

I do not personally support the protestors or the issues which demonstrators are raising. I morally and ethically do support their free speech right of expression. If they cannot do so, our time as a great nation is nearly done. The use of the word unalienable in the title of this article becomes clearer when you come to understand *the guaranteed right of free speech cannot be taken away from or given away by the possessor.*

Would you care to step forward to delete the First Amendment from the Constitution? Do you also see others we can do without? How about the Second Amendment? How about the Fourth or the Tenth Amendments?

Did you know? The Bill of Rights was introduced as promised by James Madison. The rights were ratified on December 15, 1791. On August 21, 1941 Congress authorized and requested President, F.D. Roosevelt, to issue a proclamation designating December 15,1941as Bill of Rights Day. That proclamation is still practiced annually.

Choose Wisely

Near the end of the movie, *Indiana Jones and the Last Crusade,* a character portraying extreme greed for material gain is only a single choice away from the real plum, his personal immortality. All he had to do was correctly choose the chalice from which Jesus drank from the many in front of him and everything would be his. To put it mildly, things did not turn out as he expected and the ever faithful knight who was the centuries long guardian of the chalice's on display said the only three words needed to be remembered from that film. With dignity and a touch of sorrow he said "He chose…poorly".

Another example of choosing poorly can be found in the biblical story of why the Jews were forced to wander in the desert for forty years. According to what I have read, Joshua and Caleb were selected along with ten other men to explore the Promised Land to give a report to Moses and the people. The explorers were gone for 40 days. Ten of the men saw only potential troubles, and possible failure. Joshua and Caleb tried to get the people to believe that the same Lord that got them out of Egypt would keep them safe. God, in this story became angry because the people did not trust him to do what he said he would do.

For their wickedness and ungratefulness, "God judged the people of Israel by making them wait 40 years to enter the land" which had been chosen for them. He promised that every person 20 years old or older would die in the wilderness with two exceptions. Caleb and Joshua would survive. ("Caleb son of Jephunneh and Joshua son of Nun") This curse or promise came true and Joshua led the people across the Jordan River into the Promised Land after the death of Moses forty years later. At least two men of the twelve indeed chose wisely.

Is there a parallel story in the nation called The United States of America? I really do not know. Written history does, however, speak of a man named John Winthrop who preached a sermon from the deck of a ship named Arbella that directed the listener to visualize a "City upon a hill". Clearly a city on a hill cannot be hidden. In his sermon, Winthrop clearly expressed our nations "exceptionalism" and our sociopolitical separation and superiority when it is compared to the Old World and that world is indeed watching us still.

As Ronald Reagan said in his farewell address to the nation (1/11/89), "I've spoken of the Shining City all my political life" … "God-blessed, and teeming with people of all kinds living in harmony and peace; a city with free ports that hummed with commerce and creativity. And if there had to be city walls, the walls had doors and the doors were open to anyone with the will and the heart to get here."

President-elect John F. Kennedy said, in an address to the Massachusetts Legislature on January 9, 1961 I have been guided by the standard John Winthrop set before his shipmates on the flagship Arabella [sic] 331 years ago, as they, too, faced the task of building a government on a new and perilous frontier. "We must always consider, he said, that we shall be as a city upon a hill -- the eyes of all people are truly upon us—and our governments, in every branch, at every level, national, State, and local, must be as a city upon a hill – constructed and inhabited by men aware of their grave trust and their great responsibilities.

Carefully note that neither of these modern day presidents spoke of this nation as a democracy. It is not. It is a constitutional republic. Those who would have you to believe that our constitution provided for democracy are historically mistaken.

"A democracy is an assurance of mob rule where minority factions lose their liberty through legislation and when power is consolidated over the subdued masses." James Madison wrote about this in The Federalist Papers #10. Madison also added "the ancient democracies never possessed one good feature of government. Their very character was tyranny."

John Adams our 2nd President stated "Democracy, while it lasts, is more bloody than either aristocracy or monarchy. Remember, democracy never lasts long. It soon wastes, exhausts and murders itself. There is never a democracy that did not commit suicide."

Abraham Lincoln our 16th President stated "America will never be destroyed from the outside. If we falter and lose our freedoms, it will be because we destroyed ourselves."

History has taught us and continues to teach us that it is "We the People" who must and will choose to save or destroy our nation. It is our responsibility to vote and to choose wisely. We are the latest people to live in the shining city on the hill and there is much for us to trust in our constitution and our inalienable guaranteed rights. Success and failure for future generations still remain in our hands. Consider carefully which of the two candidates before us will prove to be the best for the lifeblood of our remarkable nation.

Thanks to the editor of our local newspaper, this article became available to my fellow citizens on Monday, November 7, 2016. Yes, this is the same editor whom you met in the forward to this book. No, we do not always see eye to eye nor should we but we respect each other's opinions and that is about as good as it gets.

About the Author

Del has always been an avid reader of almost everything but he has recently turned to history and in particular our nation's foundation documents for a better understanding of the issues at play today. It is there that he discovered his inner desire to share his observations and values with those who felt their voice and values would make no difference. It is in his searching and learning that he continues to rediscover what made America great and the envy of the world.

Hoosier transplants living in Michigan, he and his wife raised two children. In the empty nest, he and his wife continue to enjoy the forty plus years of living in their forest home enjoying Michigan's four seasons and the slower life style common to Michigan's Lower Peninsula.

Alpena Co. Library
211 N. 1st Ave.
Alpena, MI 49707

Made in the USA
Middletown, DE
24 December 2016